# America's Cup From the Fifty-Yard Line

### Capt. Walter W. Jaffee

## The Glencannon Press

El Cerrito
2015

This book is copyright © 2014.

Published by The Glencannon Press
P.O. Box 1428, El Cerrito, CA 94530
Tel. 800-711-8985, Fax. 510-528-3194
www.glencannon.com

First printing.

The photo on the front cover shows the Oracle team crossing the finish line in the final race, winning the cup. The photo on the back cover is of the America's cup trophy. Both courtesy of the *San Francisco Chronicle*.

ISBN 978-1-889901-61-9

Library of Congress Cataloging-in-Publication Data on request.

# Dedication

To the crew of the *Jeremiah O'Brien*.
Without your dedication our ship would be
but a memory.

Other works by the same author.

Non-fiction:
*The Last Mission Tanker*
*The* Lane Victory, *the Last Victory Ship in War and in Peace*
*The Last Liberty, the Biography of the SS* Jeremiah O'Brien
*Appointment in Normandy*
*The Track of the* Golden Bear, *the Training Ships of*
*California Maritime Academy*
*The Presidential Yacht* Potomac
*Heritage of the Sea, the Training Ships of Maine  Maritime*
*Academy*
*Steel Shark in the Pacific, USS* Pampanito *SS 383*
*Recipes From a Coal-fired Stove*
*The Liberty Ships From A (*A.B. Hammond*) to Z (*Zona Gale*)*
SS Jeremiah O'Brien, *The History of a Liberty Ship from the*
*Battle of the Atlantic to the 21st Century*
*The Victory Ships From A (*Aberdeen Victory*) to Z*
*(*Zanesville Victory*)*
*The Tankers From A (*A.W. Peake*) to Z (*Zephyrhills*)*
*The Freighters From A (*Adabelle Lykes*) to Z (*Zoella Lykes*)*
*The Troopships and Passenger Liners From A*
*(*Admiral C.F. Hughes*) to Z (*United States*)*
*The Tugboats From A (*A.G. Wells*) to Z (*USS Zuni*)*

Fiction
*Union Gold* (as Mark West)
*Fort Ross* (as Mark West)

Editor
*The Glencannon Encyclopedia*
*The Diogenes Club Speaks* (co-editor)
*The Sherlock Holmes Illustrated Cyclopedia of Nautical*
*Knowledge*

Contributor
*Naval Warfare, An International Encyclopedia* [VMI
Encyclopedia of Naval History]

# ACKNOWLEDGMENTS

A special thank you to Stanley Jacobsen, without whose talents as a researcher, this book would be greatly lacking in detail, substance and illustrations. His determination in locating the facts is treasured. His persistence in keeping me on track is greatly valued.

And no author worth his salt would succeed without the hard work of a good editor/proofreader/question asker. Someone to inquire, "What about this?" or simply say, "This doesn't make sense." My thanks to Ellen for all that and more.

My sincere thanks to Bob Bliss, Pat Burke, Hal Drummond, Pat Dupes-Matsumoto, Wilma Fox, Linda Greig, Ellen Phillips and Dave Winter, for their contributions to this effort.

Many others donated snapshots, provided stories and shared their America's Cup experiences. My thanks to all of you. Your contributions were a great help.

A special note of thanks to the *San Francisco Chronicle* for allowing me to reproduce portions of articles, maps and photographs.

Finally a note of appreciation to Adm. Tom Patterson, who made the S.S. *Jeremiah O'Brien* possible as a living museum ship. In this case, his leadership was truly conspicuous by its absence.

# CONTENTS

# FOREWORD

Located in the heart of Fisherman's Wharf at pier 45 in San Francisco, the Liberty ship S.S. *Jeremiah O'Brien* had a unique position in the America's Cup races of 2013 — front row center. When that announcement was made at a volunteer crew meeting by Carl Nolte, chairman of the National Liberty Ship Memorial, we were electrified. Visions of mobs of people swarming aboard to watch the races swept the audience. And, in most of our minds, "mobs of people" translated to dollars and dollars meant our operating museum ship could be assured of continuing into the forseeable future.

Conjecture had us anchoring at the edge of the race course, with 800 or 900 paying passengers eager to see each contest. Several races were planned, plus all the pre- and post-race crowds. We, like most of San Francisco, looked on it as a gift; a chance to show the world community what San Francisco, and in our case the S.S. *Jeremiah O'Brien*, could do, hosting a world famous event. It would reaffirm our positions as the "can do" city and ship.

Such is the stuff of dreams. But dreams don't always jibe with reality. Reality deals with costs, egos, politics, a sense of entitlement, media, racing rules and regulations, naivete and countless other factors that make the end result far different than anyone could imagine.

First there is the America's Cup race itself. One of the oldest sporting events in history. To understand America's Cup 2013, it's helpful to know the history leading up to that competition …

W.W.J.
El Cerrito, Calif.
2014

# PART I

# THE HISTORY OF THE AMERICA'S CUP

# 1

# THE SCHOONER *AMERICA*

In 1851 Commodore John Cox Stevens, founder and commodore of the New York Yacht Club (NYYC), formed a six-person syndicate to build a schooner to compete in yachting regattas and match races in England. The syndicate also hoped to show off American know-how in yacht building and, in the process, win a bit of money in the match races. It contracted with pilot boat designer George Steers for a 101 ft. (30.78 m.) boat based on similar vessels used commercially in New York Harbor. This vessel would be finer and faster than any pilot boat and built specifically to trounce the British.

For a builder the syndicate selected William H. Brown of Manhattan. Previously, Brown, with his designer, Steers, had produced the fastest pilot boats in New York as well as some very successful racing yachts for Commodore Stevens and his brothers, James, Edward and Robert. Brown was so anxious for the building contract, he agreed that if the new yacht was not faster than any vessel of her tonnage, whether American or British, the syndicate could refuse her and owe him nothing. He also agreed the judge of whether she met these conditions would be a member of the syndicate that contracted for her. The cost of the new yacht was projected at $30,000 (considered high at the time) and she would be ready for trials on April 1.*

On April 2 the contract was extended to May 1. On May 3 the new yacht was christened *America* and launched. Because she entered the water two days after the stipulated delivery date, the contract was renegotiated. The price was reduced to $20,000.

Capt. Dick Brown, a well-known pilot boat captain, was hired as master. Under his guidance the *America* made the crossing from New York to Le Havre, France in twenty days and "passed every vessel in sight." Provisioned and fitted out for the upcoming races and with the owners now on board (they traveled to France by steamer) she crossed the English Channel and, on July 31, anchored in the Solent, six miles below Cowes, home of the Royal Yacht Squadron, on the Isle of Wight.

As the *America* prepared to get under way the following morning, she was approached by the *Lavrock*, a fast English cutter, who offered to "escort" her up the channel. While the American yacht raised her anchor, the English boat tacked around her and, at times, simply drifted. Soon the morning breeze increased to five or six knots, the crew of *America* raised her sails and the unofficial race was on. The American boat quickly worked to windward of the English yacht's wake and gained speed. She was leading by a quarter of a mile when the two yachts arrived at Cowes.

This first trial race had both good and bad results. It proved to the English just how far advanced American yacht building

---

* The caption on a wood cut engraving showing the *America* on the building ways at the William H. Brown Shipyard stated, "If she beats them she is to be paid for by the club; if she is beaten, she is then to be given up to them as a forfeit." Apparently this early notion of "winner or loser take all" was soon forgotten. It was never mentioned again.

*The racing yacht* America, *under full sail, date unknown.* U.S. Naval History and Heritage Command.

was. However, the shock waves that went through the English yachting establishment squelched the interest of anyone who might be willing to bet with the Americans on the coming races. According to the *London Times*, it was similar to the "appearance of a sparrowhawk ... among a flock of woodpigeons."

The *America* then tried to enter two races, but was disqualified from both. In each case she showed up on the courses anyway and, although starting miles behind the acknowledged entrants, was first over the finish line. Finally she was accepted as challenger in the Royal Yacht Squadron's annual regatta. The prize would be a bottomless, ornate, silver ewer, called the Hundred Guinea Cup.

On August 22, 1851, *America* raced against fifteen yachts in the Club's annual fifty-three-nautical-mile (98 km) regatta around the Isle of Wight. The *America* won, finishing eight minutes ahead

## THE TROPHY

*The America's Cup as it appeared circa 1900-1915.* Library of Congress.

Technically, the trophy is an elaborate sterling silver bottomless ewer, one of several off-the-shelf trophies crafted in 1848 by Garrard & Co. of London. Its design was based on a sixteenth century Italian wine jug. Henry William Paget, a member of the Royal Yacht Squadron bought one to be awarded to the winner of the Squadron's Annual Regatta around the Isle of Wight in 1851.

The trophy was originally known as the "R.Y.S. £100 Cup," a cup of a hundred British Pounds in value. The Cup was subsequently mistakenly engraved as the "100 Guinea Cup" by the America syndicate (a guinea is an old monetary unit of one pound and one shilling, now £1.05), probably because they believed that was the amount Mr. Paget paid for it. It has also been referred to as the "Queen's Cup" (although Queen Victoria was simply an observer), the Squadron Cup and even the Lipton Cup. Today, the trophy is officially known as the "America's Cup" after the 1851 winning yacht, and is affectionately called the "Auld Mug" by the sailing community. It is inscribed with names of the yachts that competed for it, and has been modified twice by adding matching bases to accommodate more names.

### *AMERICA*, AFTER THE CUP RACE

After being sold to Lord John de Blaquire on September 1, 1851, she was resold to Edward Decie in 1860 and renamed *Camilla*. She then returned to America and was purchased by the Confederacy in early 1861 for $60,000. There she was put into service as a blockade runner and dispatch boat.

Arriving at Savannah, Georgia on April 25, 1861 she was renamed *Memphis*. She then returned to England for cargo, still commanded by Edward Decie, with a Southern purchasing commission. In October 1861 she successfully ran the blockade at Jacksonville, Florida. However, it was decided that despite her speed, she lacked the cargo carrying capacity to be effective. To avoid capture she was scuttled in March 1862 at Dunn's Creek, a tributary of the St. Johns River in Florida.

In March 1862 she was raised by the Federal Navy and towed to Port Royal, South Carolina for repair and outfitting as a dispatch vessel and as part of the South Atlantic Blockading Squadron. On March 18 she was renamed and commissioned USS *America*.

She then took station in the inner line of blockaders off Charleston. From time to time she fired upon ships as they attempted to enter or escape from that port. Her first significant success came on October 13, 1862 when she captured the schooner *David Crockett*, which was trying to slip out to sea with a cargo of turpentine and rosin to be delivered at Bermuda. On January 29, 1863, she was one of the warships that cooperated in forcing the iron screw steamer *Princess Royal* aground. Boat crews from *America* assisted in refloating that valuable prize whose

*America, in the Severn River, circa 1866-1870, with the monitor Tonawanda (center) and an unidentified gunboat (left).* U.S. Naval Historical Center.

cargo included rifled artillery, small arms, ammunition, and steam engines for ironclads being constructed at Charleston. She then captured the British topsail schooner, *Antelope*, carrying a cargo of salt, on March 31, 1863.

Later in 1863 she was ordered north to the Naval Academy at Newport, Rhode Island. Four years later she was decommissioned and laid up at Annapolis, Maryland. In 1869 she was completely overhauled at the Washington Navy Yard. A year later she was fitted out for international racing at the New York Navy Yard. On August 8, 1870, she again competed for the America's Cup and finished fourth out of the fleet of nineteen entrants. In 1873 she was sold by the Navy to Major General Benjamin F. Butler.

In 1921 she was resold to Charles Foster, overhauled and presented to the Naval Academy. During her last major overhaul, work was stopped in 1941 due to the Japanese attack at Pearl Harbor. She was crushed by snow while in a boat shed at Annapolis, Maryland, when the area was hit by an unexpected blizzard on March 29, 1942. She was subsequently broken up for scrap. Her name was struck from the Naval Register on October 11, 1945.

of her nearest competitor. According to legend, Queen Victoria was watching at the finish line and asked who was second. She was told, "Ah, Your Majesty, there is no second."

Legend or not, that sums up the history of the event to this day. The losing boat in the America's Cup race quickly gets lost in the murky waters of time. The winner receives the Cup, worldwide fame and the glory of having won — at least until the next race.

There were protests from the losers, and that, too, is a continuing tradition. In this case the protests were dismissed.

Two significant factors accounted for the *America* dominating in this first cup race. First was her hull design. She had a sharp, lean, concave bow, with her maximum breadth just aft of the mainmast. Thus her underwater hull was sharp at each end, literally more streamlined. This compared with the bluff bows and long run of the British boats designed and based on the model of a "cod's head and mackerel tail." The second factor was the sails. The English sails were loosely woven of flax and set with a

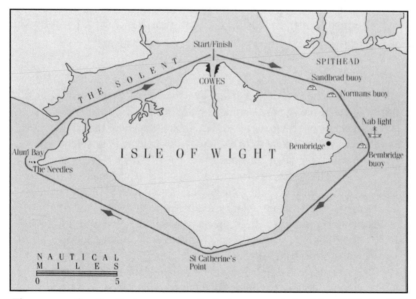

*The course for the first race ran clockwise around the Isle of Wight.* Sail Magazine.

big bag, or draft, in them. The American sails were tightly woven cotton, lighter weight and stronger, and fastened at the mast and booms, making them flatter by comparison and giving greater efficiency and driving power when going to windward.

The members of the American syndicate which owned the yacht were treated hospitably after they won, including a visit from Queen Victoria, who examined the yacht from one end to the other and charmed her owners. Six days later the *America* ran against the British *Titania* in a match race for 100 guineas. The *America* beat her opponent by almost an hour. Four days later she was sold to an Irish peer for the equivalent of $25,000. Taking in to account the cost of the boat and $3,750 in expenses, that left a profit of $1,750 plus the Cup which was valued at $500. It was the first and only time in the history of the cup that a profit was made on the venture.

The surviving members of the *America* syndicate donated the Cup via the Deed of Gift of the America's Cup to the NYYC on July 8, 1857, specifying that it be held in trust as a perpetual challenge trophy to promote friendly competition among nations.

The terms of the Deed of Gift are worth quoting, for they set the foundation for America's Cup races ever after:

> Any organized Yacht Club of any foreign country shall be entitled, through any one or more of its members, to claim the right of sailing a match for this Cup with any yacht or other vessel of not less than 30 or more than 300 tons, measured by the Custom House Rule of the country to which the vessel belongs.
>
> The parties desiring to sail for the Cup may make any match with the Yacht Club in possession of the same that may be determined upon by mutual consent; but in case of disagreement as to terms, the match shall be sailed over the usual course for the Annual Regatta of the Yacht Club in possession of the Cup, and subject to its Rules and Sailing Regulations — the challenging party being bound to give six months' notice in writing, fixing the day they wish to start. This notice to embrace the length, Custom House measurement, rig, and name of the vessel.

> It is to be distinctly understood that the Cup is to be
> the property of the Club, and not of the members thereof,
> or owners of the vessels winning it in a match; and that
> the condition of keeping it open to be sailed for by Yacht
> Clubs of all foreign countries, upon the terms above laid
> down, shall forever attach to it, thus making it perpetually
> a Challenge Cup for friendly competition between foreign
> countries.

In the decades to come there would be misunderstandings and attempts to circumvent these rules. Also, as yacht design changed there would be modifications, some in startling directions.

# 2

# ENGLAND
# CHALLENGES

Partly because of the Civil War and its effect on the world economy, it was 1869 before the New York Yacht Club was challenged for the America's Cup. In the fall of that year it received a letter from Mr. James Ashbury, owner of the British schooner *Cambria*. He offered to race his yacht against any champion American schooner selected by the New York Yacht Club and suggested that the Cup be put up as a trophy for the winner. Because his challenge did not conform to the terms of the America's Cup Deed of Gift the challenge could not be accepted. It did, however, lead to a three-year correspondence between himself and the NYYC that eventually resulted in a race for the Cup.

Ashbury was riding high on the crest of having defeated the American schooner yacht *Sappho* in a race around the Isle of Wight earlier in the year. When he received notice that the

*Artist's depiction of the* Cambria, *the first challenger for the America's Cup, underway in 1870.* www.atlantic-yachtclub.com

challenge had to be made by clubs, not individuals, Ashbury joined the Royal Thames Yacht Club; they would sponsor his boat. The NYYC then reminded him that the race had to be arranged by "mutual consent," but if the participants couldn't agree on terms, the race would be run according to the rules of the club holding the Cup.

Correspondence continued with the actual race being pushed back to 1870. Much of the discussion centered on whether the race would be run similar to the original, that is, the challenger would face a fleet of opponents (the NYYC position) or that the race would proceed according to the Deed of Gift which eliminated

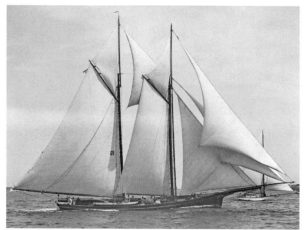

*The first challenge to the America's Cup was won by the* Magic, *a centerboarder.* www.readtiger.com

anything that transpired earlier (Ashbury's position). However when the NYYC decided the race would be held on its "inside course" off Staten Island, which required a lot of local knowledge to negotiate, Ashbury complained, then dropped the issue. He followed up with an objection to the use of centerboarders in the race.* His rationale was that centerboarders were not allowed in the original race, therefore they shouldn't be allowed in this one. He eventually dropped this issue, too.

The result was that on August 8, 1870 seventeen NYYC boats lined up with the *Cambria* at the start of the inside course. Most of the New York boats were smaller and more maneuverable than the English contender and several had that pesky adjustable centerboard keel. The winner was the centerboarder *Magic*, one of the smallest boats entered. The *America* came in fourth and *Cambria* placed eighth, although she was tenth on corrected time (A time adjustment was used to compensate for inequalities of size and design).

---

* A centerboard is a movable keel which can be raised or lowered along a boat's certerline. When lifted it decreases the boat's draft and water resistance, thus increasing the speed, especially when running downwind. Centerboarders were not up to the transatlantic run. Thus challengers which had to sail to New York for the race could not be built with them.

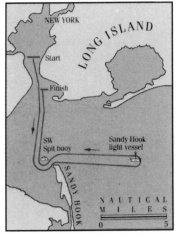

*The New York Yacht Club's inner course was used between 1870 and 1887. The total distance was about thirty-eight nautical miles.* Sail Magazine.

Ashbury and the *Cambria* remained afterward for more than a month, racing (where he lost more races than he won), joining the NYYC in its annual cruise to Newport, Rhode Island, having President Ulysses S. Grant on board the *Cambria* for breakfast and, generally serving as good will ambassador between the United States and England. But, even while cementing relationships between the two nations, he found time to order a new vessel built in England to challenge for the Cup again the following year.

The *Cambria* returned to England where she was sold into commercial service running coal between Swansea, Wales and Cork. She then spent the remainder of her career in the West African coasting trade. She was lost early in the 20th century.

*Postage stamp issued by the Solomon Islands commemorating the* Magic's *win of the 1870 America's Cup.* www.philateliemarine.fr

# 3

# ASHBURY RETURNS

A shbury's new boat was built by Michael Ratsey of Cowes, England, the same firm that built the *Cambria*. He named it *Livonia* after a Russian province in which he had made money (apparently a lot of it) building railroads. The yacht incorporated many of the design characteristics of the American schooners, including sails made of woven cotton with a total area of 18,153 square feet, the largest spread of sail ever carried by an America's Cup challenger.

Upon his return to England, the first thing Ashbury did was consult his lawyers. The second thing was to launch a storm of letters, complaints and demands at the NYYC concerning the previous race and the race to come. He objected to having to race a single boat against an entire fleet of competitors. The club, having received negative comments from local yachtsmen on just that point, asked the surviving member of the *America* syndicate,

*The* Livonia, *owned by James Ashbury, challenged for the America's Cup in 1871.* Ernle Bradford.

George L. Schuyler, his opinion. Schuyler said he felt the existing conditions (one challenger against a fleet) made the America's Cup useless as a challenge cup. In his opinion, the word "match" meant only two contestants. And the Deed of Gift clearly stated that the competition for the Cup was to be a match.

The result was on March 24, 1871, the NYYC committee resolved, "that we sail one or more representative vessels, against the same number of foreign challenging vessels."

Apparently feeling the tide in his favor, Ashbury then launched two additional demands: one, that centerboarders be excluded and, two, that a different course be chosen. He followed this up with a proposal. Holding membership in twelve yacht clubs, he wished to represent all of them. He proposed a series of twelve races with the first yacht to win seven of the twelve being declared the winner. He would sail under the flag of a different club each day and if he won the Cup it would go to the club whose colors he flew in the final race.

The NYYC waited until Ashbury arrived in New York in early October of 1871 to reply that "The Deed of Gift of the Cup carefully guards against any such sharp practice."

Ashbury responded with an even more creative proposition. He insisted that all twelve races must be sailed. If not, he would take his boat and go home. Alternatively, he would withdraw his objection to centerboarders and interpret the Deed of Gift as allowing him one race for each club he belonged to (twelve) and the first race which *Livonia* won would allow him to claim the cup for the club whose flag he was flying at the time.

After several more back and forthings between the NYYC and Ashbury, he agreed to the following terms: The Cup would be decided by a seven-race series, four races to win, three on the inside course, three on the outside course. The seventh race, if necessary, would be on the outside course. Ashbury would represent the Royal Harwich Yacht Club only. Certerboarders would be allowed.

*The NYYC outer course included an opening leg to windward.* Sail Magazine.

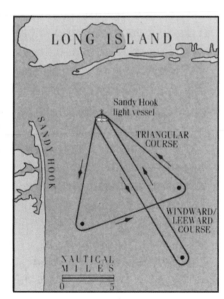

*The* Sappho *was the other co-defender in the America's Cup race of 1871.*
www.dlnhs.org

The NYYC then announced that they would choose four
boats to defend the Cup, reserving the right to choose which of
the four to pit against Ashbury on the morning of each race. By
having four yachts of different sailing characteristics, they could
pick the one best suited to the weather conditions on each day.

Ashbury again complained, but gave in when he realized it
was a take it or leave it proposition and he didn't really want to
return to England without having at least *tried* to win.

The committee named *Columbia, Sappho, Dauntless* and
*Palmer* as defenders. The *Columbia*, a centerboarder which drew
six feet with the board up and was designed for light and moderate
breezes, was chosen as the first defender. The first contest was held
on October 16. The wind was a light northwesterly. The *Columbia*
won by twenty-seven minutes, four seconds, corrected time.

Two days later the second race was held. Again the *Columbia*
was the defender, despite a freshening breeze from the southwest
which increased to a moderate gale after backing to west-north-

*The* Columbia *was co-defender of the America's Cup for the New York Yacht Club in 1871.* en.wikipedia.org

west. She won by ten minutes, thirty-three seconds, corrected time. Ashbury filed a protest over the proper way to take the turn necessary between the two legs of the race, to no avail.

Because the other three boats were out of commission on race day, the *Columbia* was again chosen for the third race. Nothing went right for her. The crew had done nothing to prepare her, a substitute sailing master had to be chosen, part of the crew were new, she lost three minutes at the start, she carried too much sail for the conditions (a fresh southwesterly), her fore-gafftopsail split, her flying jib was lost, her steering gear broke, the maintopmast staysail parted and she limped in fifteen minutes, ten seconds, behind the challenger. This was the largest margin of victory by a challenger in the history of the America's Cup.

The *Sappho* was chosen for the fourth and fifth races which she won by thirty minutes, twenty-one seconds and twenty-five minutes, twenty-seven seconds respectively. That made it United States 4, England one. The challenger was defeated.

Never one to stand still or be quiet, Ashbury went over the course again for the sixth race, claiming *Livonia* winner. On day of the seventh race the weather was so bad the starting boat couldn't get out. As no defender appeared on the course Ashbury again declared himself winner and entitled to the cup. His reasoning, imaginative to say the least, was: he won the second race by protest, the third race by sailing it, the sixth and seventh races because there were no boats on the course defending the title. Ergo it was four to three in favor of England. The NYYC did not agree and the Cup stayed where it was.

Ashbury returned home, sending out a blizzard of complaints in his wake. Some said he singlehandedly almost managed to end diplomatic relations between the United States and Great Britain. The NYYC considered him demanding, condescending and unsportsmanlike. They wanted nothing to do with him in the future.

Ashbury was later elected to Parliament and raced *Livonia* for a time. He then moved to New Zealand and became a sheep rancher.

*Columbia* ended her racing career in 1908, when she was dismasted and used as a houseboat in Brooklyn Harbor on the East River. Three years later she was rebuilt and sailed as a cruiser out of Newport News, Virginia. In 1920, she was bought by a fisherman. She was declared lost in 1923.

# 4

# O CANADA

With the English and American yachting fraternities barely speaking, the next challenge had to come from elsewhere. After five years it did, of all places, from Canada.

In April of 1876 the Royal Canadian Yacht Club (RCYC) of Toronto challenged the NYYC for the America's Cup. It was well timed. The New York Yacht Club was going through a difficult time; the second Ashbury match had left a bad taste in everyone's mouth, their membership was down and finances were weak. A world-famous yacht race would be an ideal way to commemorate the United States' centennial. In addition, such an event would boost the sport of yacht racing, just when it was needed.

The challenge was issued on behalf of a syndicate headed by Major Charles Gifford, Vice-Commodore of the RCYC. He asked that the New York club waive the six months' notice so the event could be held in July. The NYYC, with a maturing sense of responsibility toward the Deed of Gift, agreed. They also offered to sail three races rather than one. The event would be held in July with one race over the inside course, one over the outer course and the third to be decided by lot. Major Gifford also asked that the New York Club pick a single defender for the races ahead of time. This would make the race more competitive and eliminate the edge the NYYC club had in being able to select the best boat from their stable according to weather conditions on the day of each race. After some hesitation, the club agreed, by a vote of 11-5 and, in so doing, set the conditions for Cup races in the decades to come.

The challenging boat was the *Countess of Dufferin,* named for the Governor General of Ontario's wife. She was a center-board schooner designed and built by Capt. Alexander Cuthbert of Cobourg, Ontario, Canada. An experienced builder, he had designed several fast yachts for racing on the Great Lakes. The *Countess of Dufferin*'s design was based on an earlier successful

*Canada's challenger for the Cup was the* Countess of Dufferin, *modeled after earlier American racing yachts.* www.afyacht.com

vessel, the *Annie Cuthbert* (the fastest boat on Lake Ontario), which, in turn, was based on an earlier yacht, which was based on an American boat built in New Jersey. American newspapers commented that "there was nothing foreign about her. Her shape was American. Her rig was American. ...she is simply a Yankee yacht built in Canada."

Arriving in New York on July 18, 1876, the *Countess of Dufferin* went into drydock for refitting. This first view of the challenger gave American critics a chance for appraisal — and criticism. Her overall lines were pleasing. However, she was roughly built, her rigging was inefficient, her sails were baggy. According to some she was nothing more than a fresh-water boat built to race on the Great Lakes. She had a hull "as rough as a nutmeg grinder" and sails that "set like a purser's shirt on a handspike." The Canadian syndicate that sponsored her showed their lack of financial wherewithal in creating her. Clearly she suffered from economies in her rig, rigging and gear. Even the finish on her hull and decks was rough, more like a working boat than a yacht. "As rough as a down East lumber schooner," according to one writer.

Before the America's Cup races, the *Countess of Dufferin* was entered in the Brenton Reef Cup race. The best she could do over the 275-mile ocean course was to be still below the horizon after her four competitors had crossed the finish line. This brought about a request for postponement of the America's Cup races so the Canadian challenger could have a new set of sails made and modify her masts. The NYYC granted the request.

Meanwhile a defender for the Cup was chosen. She was the *Madeline*, owned by John S. Dickerson, commodore of the Brooklyn Yacht Club. In 1873 she had won every regatta in which she was entered. She was about the same size as *Countess of Dufferin* and a centerboarder.

The first race was held on August 11, 1876. For the first time in America's Cup history, the yachts began with a running start

*The* Madeline *successfully defended the America's Cup title, winning in two races.* Lawson's History of the America's Cup.

— the old practice of starting from anchor was now history. The *Madeline* won by ten minutes, fifty-nine seconds on corrected time.

The second race was held the next day in light winds. Joining in the race, but not competing, was the venerable *America*. At the end of the day the defender again won, by twenty-seven minutes, fourteen seconds. The *America* beat the challenger by nineteen minutes, nine seconds.

Following the race, due to the owners' financial difficulties the *Countess of Dufferin* was impounded at the request of her creditors. She was sold and eventually went to a Chicago yachtsman who kept her in Lake Michigan with the Chicago Yacht Club. There she was successful for several years in local races.

# 5

# CUTHBERT RETURNS

Capt. Alexander Cuthbert belonged to the Bay of Quinte
Yacht Club of Belleville, Ontario, Canada. He designed
and built a sloop (single mast, fore-and-aft rigged), the
*Atalanta.* The Bay of Quinte club challenged for the Cup on his
behalf. Apparently, Cuthbert thought he could do better than the
syndicate that offered the challenge in the previous competition.

Cuthbert was sadly mistaken. Built in haste, without proper
funding, the *Atalanta* was not at all close to her proper racing
trim. She was launched on September 17, 1881, almost too late for
the yachting season. Knowing that a trip down the St. Lawrence
would take too long, Cuthbert took his boat to Oswego, New York.
There his crew unshipped her rigging and spars and shifted her
ballast to one side so she would list enough to pass through the
locks. She was then towed to Albany by mules, before she could

*A print of the* Atalanta, *showing her centerboard raised, but protruding slightly.* Sail Museum.

be refitted and sail down the Hudson to New York. Perhaps as a tribute to Cuthbert's determination, the NYYC agreed to delay the race until early November.

Meanwhile, the defending club, having never faced a sloop before, began a frantic search to locate one. The fastest sloop in America was the *Arrow*. However, she was owned by a non-member. Her builder, David Kirby, offered to build an even faster one for them. The offer was accepted and soon a new sloop, the *Pocahontas*, was launched. The club ran her against three other

*The* Mischief *underway in light airs with a full set of sails working.* www.jsjohnston.org

potential defenders, *Hildegard, Gracie* and *Mischief,* in a series of three races. She was horribly slow and quickly withdrawn, earning the nickname "Pokey."

Of the remaining three, *Mischief,* with her unusual iron hull, was chosen to defend the Cup. *Gracie* was a bit faster, but would have to spot the challenger eight minutes in time allowance, whereas *Mischief* would concede only three minutes. The fact that the latter boat was owned by NYYC member Joseph R. Busk, an Englishman, upset some of the members, but she was chosen nonetheless.

As race day approached Cuthbert and his crew worked frantically to get their boat ready. In the end they ran out of money and time. When the *Atalanta* arrived at the starting line on November 9 her hull was still rough, her reworked sails looked baggy, and most of her crew were amateur fresh-water sailors from the Bay of Quinte club. She lost the first race by more than thirty-one minutes. The following day she lost the second race by nearly forty-two minutes. Ironically, the *Gracie* ran in both races, not as a competitor, but just for the fun of it, and, starting ten minutes late, crossed the finish line before the *Mischief* in each case.

Capt. Cuthbert returned to Canada after promising he would be back in the spring with his boat improved. But the NYYC had enough of him. It formally handed the Cup back to George Schuyler, the remaining member of *America*'s syndicate. He reconveyed the Cup back to the club in 1882 with a new Deed of Gift.

The new document modified the existing Deed of Gift with the following conditions:

1. Only a single yacht would be named defender.
2. Challenges would be accepted only from clubs that had their annual regatta on the sea, or an arm of the sea.
3. Challenging vessels had to reach the port where the races were scheduled under sail and on their own bottoms.
4. No defeated challenger could challenge again until another challenger, or two years, had intervened.

Cuthbert and the Ontario Canadians were now excluded. The NYYC sat back and waited for the next challenge.

A year later *Atalanta* was sailing on Lake Ontario. In 1883 she sailed to Chicago to race in the Fisher Cup which she took back to Bay of Quinte. She held that trophy until 1886. In 1896 she was partly burned then sold and taken to Chicago where she was rebuilt with higher topsides and flush decks. She was last seen in New Orleans in 1900.

# 6

# THE ENGLISH CUTTERS

With the Ashbury affair all but forgotten after fourteen years, the NYYC welcomed a new challenge from the English in 1885. On February 26, J. Beavor Webb, a yacht designer, forwarded two challenges. He proposed that his first challenger, the *Genesta**, race between August 20 and September 1, and if she were beaten, his second, the *Galatea*, be allowed to challenge before September 17. The former yacht was owned by Sir Richard Sutton, a member of the Royal Yacht Squadron, the other was owned by Lt. William Henn, R.N. of the Royal Northern Yacht Club.

The *Genesta* challenge was accepted while that of the *Galatea* was postponed for a year, with the understanding that it

---

\* She was built with steel framing and oak planking, being the first such composite vessel to sail for the Cup.

*Although the* Genesta *lost, she made the races close enough to greatly increase public interenst in the sport.* www.pinterest.com

would be accepted if the NYYC successfully defended the first challenge. The first match would be made up of three races: one on the inside course, one on a triangular course in open water, and the third, if necessary, on a twenty-mile course off Sandy Hook.

Negotiations over details of the upcoming event lasted several months and were noteworthy because of their spirit of cordiality and good sportsmanship.

One problem remained. Where would the New York Yacht Club find a "cutter" to defend the Cup? A notice was sent out to all United States yacht clubs, announcing trials for the upcoming race. They would be open to any single-mast vessel with at least a sixty-foot waterline belonging to "any duly organized yacht club in the United States, with the condition that any vessel taking part therein shall be subject to selection by the committee in charge as the representative of the NYYC in the coming races for the America's Cup."

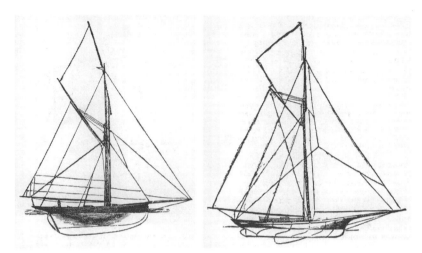

*The differences between the English cutter, left, and the American sloop, right, can be seen in these drawings. The cutter has a deep, angled keel and a plumb bow. The sloop has a straight keel, centerboard, and a sharper bow.* Australian Seacraft.

A syndicate was formed in Boston to build such a yacht, the *Puritan*, which was launched on May 26, 1885. She was entered as an Eastern Yacht Club vessel. The owners were determined that their boat would outsail and outshine anything previously built. The main cabin was finished in mahogany and pine, had two mahogany sideboards, large lounges, a ladies' cabin "beautifully furnished with every convenience," and two staterooms. There was also room below for the captain and two mates, a roomy galley, lavatory and forecastle with bunks for a crew of eighteen. With so many extras, it was a wonder she could race at all. But, race she did, beating out three other contenders, and was chosen as defender.

The *Puritan* went onto the NYYC list under the name of Edward Burgess, her designer, who flew his pennant during the trials and the Cup races. The boat was managed by Gen. Charles J. Paine, a member of the NYYC, and was entered under his name for the match. Thus the fiction was maintained that the America's Cup trophy would be challenged for by one yacht club against another.

*The* Puritan *won both races, despite being poked in the mainsail by the challenger's bowsprit.* www.jsjohnston.org

The 1885 match was especially noteworthy because good sportsmanship prevailed. At the start of the first race the sailing master of the *Puritan* misjudged his time and distance, causing the *Genesta* to ram her bowsprit through the American yacht's mainsail. The race committee ruled the *Puritan* out and explained to Sir Richard Sutton, the *Genesta*'s owner, that he could claim the race simply by sailing over the course alone. Sir Richard replied, "We are very much obliged to you, but we don't want it in that way. We want a race; we don't want a walkover." The American yacht's owners offered to pay for all repairs to the challenger, Sir Richard declined the offer.

The *Puritan* won the next two complete races. The first was held on the inner course and she came in sixteen minutes and nineteen seconds ahead of the challenger, despite the *Genesta* nearly catching her several times in unpredictable winds and bothersome tides. The challenger led at the beginning of the second race and it was close until the defender got a better angle toward the finish and put on a burst of speed that carried her across one minute and thirty-eight seconds ahead of the challenger.

Sir Richard's gallantry and the closeness of the races regained the public's interest in the Cup. Sir Richard was made an honorary member of the NYYC and good relations between English and American yachtsmen were restored.

After the Cup races, the *Genesta* won the Brenton Reef Cup, the Cape May Challenge Cup, and, upon returning to Britain, the first Round Britain Race in 1887, covering the 1,590-mile (2,560 km) course in twelve days, sixteen hours, and fifty-nine minutes. She was sold and converted to a yawl by the 1890s, and was finally broken up in 1900.

# 7

# MRS. HENN'S MENAGERIE

As previously agreed, the NYYC formally accepted the *Galetea* challenge of Lt. William Henn. The terms and conditions for the match were generally the same as the previous challenge.

Gen. Charles J. Paine ordered a new vessel from Edward Burgess, an "improved *Puritan.*" Launched as the *Mayflower*, she required some breaking in, but when everything was finely tuned she proved better than the *Puritan*. After two trial races, in which she beat the *Puritan,* the *Priscilla* and the *Atlantic*, the America's Cup committee chose her as defender.

The *Galetea* carried opulence to a new level. She was made of steel and appeared to be quite formidable. However, inside she looked more like a Victorian mansion than a racing yacht, with several heavy tables, mirrors, paintings, leopard-skin rugs, potted

*The interior of the Galetea had all the accoutrements and style(?) of a Victorian mansion. Presumably that is Lt. Henn holding a document.* The America's Cup, an Informal History.

palms and a fireplace in the saloon. Her owners, Lt. Henn and his wife, lived aboard.

Henn retired from the Royal Navy when he was 28, setting out to spend the rest of his life sailing for pleasure. He married a financially well-endowed lady with similar ambitions. She supplied the money for the vessel and decided on her furnishing and the passenger manifest. This included: dogs, cats, a raccoon and a monkey named Peggy. According to one report, Peggy helped the crew make and lower sail, pulling on a halyard like a seasoned sailor. Whenever *Galetea* pulled ahead in a race, she would run out on the bowsprit and jump up and down.

The monkey didn't get a lot of exercise in 1885. Lt. Henn entered the yacht in fifteen races and lost every one.

The first race for the America's Cup in 1886 was won by the *Mayflower*, twelve minutes and two seconds ahead of the challenger. The second race was again won by the defender, this time by twenty-nine minutes and nine seconds.

Lt. Henn took the defeat gracefully. He was well liked and regarded as a friendly boat owner, but not considered much of a racer.

*Mrs. Henn as she appeared at the time of the Cup races.* The America's Cup, an Informal History.

The *Galetea* won the Queen's Jubilee Cup Royal Nova Scotia Yacht Squadron Regatta in Halifax on August 20, 1887. From 1888 until 1894, Mr. and Mrs. Henn lived aboard, in Britain. Following Lt. Henn's death in 1894, Mrs. Henn continued to live aboard until her death in 1911. In January 1912, the boat was sold for scrap and broken up.

When Peggy, the monkey, died, she was buried with full honors: draped in a Union Jack, with four skippers from nearby yachts serving as pall-bearers.

*Mrs. Henn's pets included dogs, cats, a raccoon, and Peggy, a monkey.* The America's Cup, an Informal History.

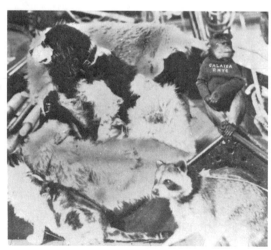

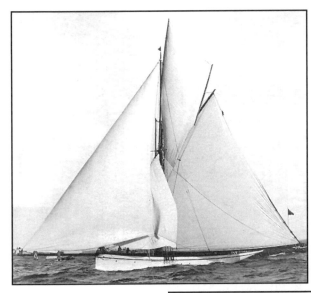

*The* Galetea *challenged for the Cup in 1886.* forum. woodenboat.com

*The* Mayflower *defended, and won, the America's Cup in 1886.* www.sandroferuglio. com

# 8

# BAGPIPES
# AND
# SCOTS WHISKY

S hortly after the *Galatea-Mayflower* race the NYYC received a letter from a syndicate headed by James Bell, vice
commodore of the Royal Clyde Yacht Club of Scotland.
He wrote of their intention to challenge for the America's Cup
in 1887. It was an informal, friendly announcement which the
RCYC considered the beginning of negotiations toward a formal
challenge which would arrive in time to schedule the races for
September. The New York club's response was to simply say that
when the challenge arrived "in proper form" it would be considered. With the response, they included a copy of the second Deed
of Gift.

Trying again, the Scottish syndicate endeavored to at least
reach some understanding about the size of the boats. That also
failed. The syndicate went ahead on its own, building their boat

in secrecy and delaying the challenge until March, just under the six-month deadline.

The Scottish designer was George L. Watson, considered the best British designer at the time. He had spent a year in America, studying the best U.S. yachts and thought he could blend the outstanding features of American sloops with those of English cutters to develop an unbeatable design. Their boat, the *Thistle*, was built by D. & W. Henderson at Patrick on the Clyde and launched on April 26, 1887. She was covered with canvas to prevent anyone from seeing her design. This aroused the interest of the press to such a degree that Watson began misleading them, passing off the plans of other vessels as those of the *Thistle*.

*The Scottish yacht and challenger* Thistle *was built in secrecy and covered with canvas to prevent the competition from learning the details of her construction. This photo was taken on September 17, 1887.* Library of Congress.

Once the yacht began racing she did quite well, beating the *Genesta* and winning eleven of fifteen races against the best of the English cutters. She then sailed across the Atlantic under the command of Capt. John Barr, considered the best skipper Scotland could produce.

Soon after the yacht arrived in New York, a newspaper hired a diver to examine her hull. The water was very muddy on the day

*The defender* Volunteer *is shown turning during the race on September 27, 1887.* Library of Congress.

of the dive and when the resulting drawing was published it was so inaccurate, Bell remarked the paper's owner would feel like shooting the diver when the yacht's true form was revealed.

Meanwhile, the Scottish syndicate members arrived by steamer, bringing with them bagpipers and a supply of Scotch, which they declared they would drink from the America's Cup (apparently they didn't know it had no bottom) when they won.

A defending yacht had been built by Paine and Burgess, the *Volunteer*. She was a steel-hulled sloop, built in just sixty-six days. Because she was put together so quickly, her finish was quite rough. Her master was Capt. Henry Clayton Haff ("Hank Haff"), a veteran yachtsman from Long Island. The *Volunteer*'s first races were victories and she even easily beat the *Mayflower* and the *Puritan*.

The Scots' efforts at misdirection were matched by those of the Yankees. While practicing one day before the match, it was noticed that the *Thistle* was keeping pace with the *Volunteer* just outside the course. The wind was increasing, but rather than lower the topsail, the captain of the American boat ordered it to be luffed during some heavy gusts in the hopes that the challenger would think her unusually stable and add ballast to match her. That's what they did and it noticeably slowed the *Thistle*.

*The* Thistle *in drydock, probably after the America's Cup Race.* www.jsjohnston.org.

On September 22 the challenger and defender were officially measured. The *Thistle* was found to be 1.46 feet longer than reported by the designer. This lead to a demand for disqualification, which was denied.

A large fleet of spectators crowded the inside course for the first race on September 27, making it difficult to maneuver. The race was a walkaway for the defender with *Volunteer* winning by nineteen minutes, twenty-three seconds corrected time. The challenger's owners had their boat's bottom swept after the race, to be sure she had not picked up something that was slowing her down. The second race, held on September 30, was also won by the defender in eleven minutes, forty-eight seconds.

The bagpipers remained silent.

The *Thistle*'s owners presumably drowned their sorrows in the scotch.

The *Thistle* sailed for home in October. She was later sold to the German Emperor, who raced her for several years under the name *Meteor*. In 1895 she was given to the German Navy as a school yacht and renamed *Comet*. She was broken up in 1921.

The *Volunteer* sailed and raced for many years and was broken up in 1911.

# 9

# THE IRISH CHALLENGE

Secrecy in the design and construction of the *Thistle* rankled with the New York Yacht Club. Because of it they only had six months to design, build and try out their boat defending the Cup. As far as they were concerned that was cutting it too close. Their reaction was to, yet again, revise the Deed of Gift.

A committee was appointed to adjust the deed to their liking and published the revision a month after the Cup race against Scotland. The NYYC thought they had merely closed a few of the loopholes and condensed some of the language, in the interest of assuring that the deed and the event would survive, should they ever lose the cup.

But, the new deed was received by the yachting world as the end of everything they held dear. The document was more than five times as long as the original 1857 deed. Clearly it was drafted by a lawyer, and, in the words of one critic, it "read like a mortgage." Another said "the Cup seemed no longer to be a trophy designed for 'friendly competition.' It seemed to have lost what, essentially, it had long represented: the irrepressible elements of the wind and the sea and the fellowship of sport for its own sake. Challengers now had to navigate cautiously through 'parties of the first and second part' and equivalent hazards."

Even so, most of the criticism was leveled against the content of the document, rather than the form. Challengers would now have to give ten months' notice rather than six. In addition they would have to submit the name, rig and dimensions of the challenging vessel: load waterline length, beam at the load waterline, extreme beam and draft. Once announced, those dimensions could not be exceeded. Another provision eliminated time allowances, used to adjust for differences in boats' dimensions. In effect, once the challenger submitted the characteristics of their boat, the NYYC had ten months in which to develop a yacht that could beat her.

In reality the NYYC never insisted on more than the waterline length in advance, and the ten months' notice was normally waived.

Additional requirements of the new document included the stipulation that all races would be held on "ocean courses, free from headlands" and "practicable in all parts of vessels of 22 feet draft of water." Centerboarders would always be allowed to compete, and any challenger that won the Cup would have to agree, in writing, to abide by all provisions of the deed before taking it over.

All the above having been said, when asked for a clarification from the Royal London Yacht Club six months later, the NYYC replied with a resolution stating that the "mutual consent" clause would allow the parties involved to ignore most of the new clauses and the terms under which the last three challenges were raced had been satisfactory. In other words, mutual consent could obviate everything in the new Deed of Gift.

Enter Windham Thomas Wyndham-Quin, fourth Earl of Dunraven. An Irish peer, Lord Dunraven came with impressive credentials. While active in politics he also found time to work as war correspondent for the London *Daily Telegraph* during the Franco-Prussian War of 1870-1871. Although involved in steeplechasing, his main love was sailing. He wrote a three-volume book, *Self-instruction in the Practice and Theory of Navigation,* held a Master's Certificate in seamanship, and had helped design several yachts. His first challenge was received on March 19, 1889, from the Royal Yacht Squadron.

*Lord Dunraven had an impact (in many ways) upon the America's Cup and New York Society.* www.flikr.com

A committee was formed to arrange details, one of which was that the Royal Yacht Squadron agree to abide by the deed if they won the Cup. This they refused to do. Lord Dunraven's views on the matter were expressed in a letter to the committee the following year. He objected to: the change from six months notice to ten months notice, the requirement to furnish his boat's exact dimensions, and the ambiguity of the mutual consent clause. The challenge was dropped.

In November 1892 he challenged again, naming his boat, the *Valkyrie II,* designed by George L. Watson, and giving its load waterline as 85 feet. Eventually terms were worked out, ignoring most of the revised deed of trust because of the mutual consent clause. In the end the load-waterline measurement was the only one required, with the stipulation that the defender could be no more than 2 percent longer than the challenger. If the Royal Yacht Squadron won, it agreed that any subsequent challenge would be accepted according to the 1887 Deed of Gift.

For a new defending yacht the NYYC turned to Nathaniel Greene Herreshoff of Bristol, Rhode Island. Educated at the Massachusetts Institute of Technology, Herreshoff and his brother had

Nathaniel Herreshoff designed and built six America's Cup defenders. www.engineeringthephd.com

built launches and small steamers as the Herreshoff Manufacturing Company and, in the 1870s produced several small catamarans and sloops. He would design and build six Cup defenders between 1893 and 1920.

Herreshoff was commissioned to design and build two potential defenders: the *Vigilant*, a centerboarder, and the *Colonia*, a keel boat. The syndicates funding the two boats were made up of some of the world's richest men, including two Morgans (J.P. and E.D.), two Belmonts and three Vanderbuilts. During trials the two boats finished one race in a dead heat, the first ever in trial races.

The *Valkyrie II* arrived in New York on September 22, 1893. She quickly proved herself a formidable challenger. Lord

*The* Vigilant *successfully defended the America's Cup in 1893. This photo was taken during one of the races.* jsjohnston.org

*The* Valkyrie II
*challenged for the*
*America's Cup*
*in 1893.* www.
jsjohnston.org

Dunraven had a similar effect on New York society and his style of dressing was often imitated by the young men of the day.

In the first attempted race, the *Valkyrie II* threw a scare into the ranks of the NYYC. She was twenty-six minutes, twenty seconds ahead of the *Vigilant* at the outer mark before the race was cancelled because the wind completely died. The first full race was won by the defender in a moderate breeze by five minutes and forty-eight seconds, corrected time. She won the second race by ten minutes and thirty-five seconds.

The third race, held on Friday, October 13, was a near thing. In a brisk wind, the *Valkyrie II* led slightly around the first mark. During the return leg, both boats crowded on canvas. The *Valkyrie II*'s spinnaker ripped. A second, lighter one was run up only to meet the same fate. While the third was being hoisted the *Vigilant* passed her and held on to win by forty seconds corrected time.

Lord Dunraven did not accept defeat gracefully. He complained that the races were not a fair test under the wind conditions. He groused about the interference from steamers loaded with spectators. He grumbled that his boat was out of trim and too light to keep her within the stipulated waterline.

Nonetheless, he would be back.

On July 5, 1894 the *Valkyrie II* collided with A.D. Clarke's cutter yacht *Satanita* at the Mud Hook Regatta on the Firth of Clyde, killing one crewman. The *Valkyrie II* broke up and sank nine minutes later.

In 1894 the *Vigilant* was bought by Howard Gould and became the first America's Cup defender to sail in Europe for the British yachting season. In sixteen races against the *Britannia*, she was beaten twelve times. She raced in the defender trials for the 1895 America's Cup won by the *Defender*. From 1896 to 1910 she had six owners the last of whom was William Iselin who sailed her from 1906 until 1910. She was broken up at a New London junkyard in 1910.

# 10

# DUNRAVEN DONE WRONG

In October of 1894 Lord Dunraven challenged again through the Royal Yacht Squadron. As negotiations began for the details of the coming event, the Squadron let it be known they were still opposed to strictly maintaining the deed if they should win. They said they didn't really care about the Cup itself and the New York club could keep the silly trophy. The NYYC replied firmly that the RYS could not reject it, if they won. Eventually the challenging club agreed to these terms.

Nathaniel Herreshoff was again commissioned to design and build a defender. The syndicate ordering the new yacht included the millionaires William K. Vanderbuilt, E.D. Morgan and C. Oliver Iselin. The new vessel, named *Defender*, was launched in secrecy on June 29, 1895.

The *Defender* was a sloop with a fin keel, the first non-centerboarder to defend the Cup. Built of bronze, steel and aluminum

*The defending yacht in the 1895 America's Cup match was, appropriately, the Defender.* en.wikipedia.org

to save weight, she was about seventeen tons lighter than she would have been if made of conventional materials. Her light weight made her a temperamental boat to handle throughout her racing career.

Dunraven again turned to George L. Watson for his challenger, the *Valkyrie III*. Her 26.2-foot beam was the widest ever seen in an America's Cup match. She looked a lot like the defender and the two vessels were considered evenly matched in design and performance.

During the negotiations leading up to the match, added emphasis was placed on measurement. The yachts were to be measured "with all weights on board to be carried in a race." A clause was added that required remeasurement whenever a boat was modified in any way that would change her waterline length.

Dunraven was of the opinion that the load waterline points would be marked on the hull of each boat. On September 6, 1895, the day before the first race, he wrote that the committee should "take every precaution that the vessels sail on their measured load waterline length," to guard against "alterations"

*The challenging vessel was Lord Dunraven's* Valkyrie III. www. jsjohnston.org

being made "without the owner's knowledge, and without possibility of detection." A special committee was appointed to mark the load waterline of both boats, but the *Valkyrie III* had already been measured and could not be brought back in before the race, therefore neither boat was marked.

Just before the race Dunraven filed a charge against the NYYC's syndicate accusing the defender of sailing the race three or four feet beyond their vessel's given waterline length. In other words he claimed the NYYC added ballast to give them an edge. In short, they cheated. Once he was beaten by the *Defender*, by eight minutes and forty-nine seconds, he said the situation must be corrected or he would "discontinue racing." He asked for re-measurement.

Both boats were remeasured the following day. The *Defender* showed a 1/8 inch difference in her waterline, the *Valkyrie III* 1/16 of an inch.

As the yachts maneuvered into position to start the second race, a large steamer, the *City of Yorktown*, crossed in their path. The defender went astern of the steamer, the challenger crossed ahead. The result was the two yachts converged with the defender having the right of way to leeward. In order not to get to the

*A view from the after deck of Capt. Uriah Rhodes and crew of the* Defender *practicing in 1899.* www.allposters.com

starting line before the gun, the *Valkyrie III* turned toward the *Defender*. A shackle on the end of her main boom caught in the *Defender*'s starboard topmast shroud. The shroud sprang out of the spreader and her topmast sagged to leeward. The *Defender* immediately raised a protest flag, which the committee answered with a pennant. Contrary to the rules and tradition, the *Valkyrie III* continued for the finish line. The *Defender* continued the race, making repairs while she ran, crossing forty-seven seconds behind the challenger.

Afterward the committee ruled in favor of the *Defender*, awarding it the race.

C. Oliver Iselin, representing the NYYC syndicate offered to resail the race, but Dunraven refused. Others suggested that the committee order the race resailed, but they explained they could only order a rematch when neither party was at fault.

That evening Dunraven wrote the committee that he would not race again under the same conditions, that is, crowding by the spectator boats. The NYYC created yet another special committee to consult with him. He agreed to sail if it would declare the race void if either boat was interfered with. The committee had no such authority and continued with preparations for the next day's race.

On September 12 the spectators steered well clear of the starting area. As the *Valkyrie III* closed in on the starting line it was apparent something was amiss. She was under jib and mainsail only and had not made any of the normal pre-race preparations. When the warning gun was fired to approach the starting line she made no move to gain on the defender. She followed slowly, about a minute and a half later. As soon as she crossed, she came about, lowered her racing pennant and raised the burgee of the NYYC. She then called her tug and was towed back to port. Dunraven had quit!

The *Defender* finished the race alone, retaining the Cup.

The controversy and letters continued long after Lord Dunraven returned home, centering mostly on Dunraven's allegation of cheating. On December 27, 1895 a five-day inquiry was held at the NYYC. Dunraven attended with his admiralty lawyers. The New York club was equally manned. After much discussion the inquiry found Dunraven's charges to be entirely unfounded. No apology was received from him and in February of the follow-

*Badge commemorating the event.*
www.oldpoliticals.com

ing year he was expelled, by a vote of 39 to 1, from his honorary membership of the NYYC.

The Earl of Dunraven was never heard from again, but the memory of his lack of sportsmanship lasted a long time.

The *Valkyrie III* was broken up in 1901.

Following the contest, the *Defender* was towed to New Rochelle where she remained for another four years without sailing. She was rebuilt to race trials against the 1899 America's Cup defender, *Columbia*. The *Defender* was broken up in 1901.

# 11

# SIR THOMAS
# AND THE
# TEA CLIPPER(S)

O n August 6, 1898 a challenge was received from the
Royal Ulster Yacht Club on behalf of Sir Thomas John-
stone Lipton. Unknown in yachting circles, Lipton had
a worldwide reputation with tea drinkers. Born into poverty,

*Sir Thomas Lipton was known*
*throughout the world for his*
*teas.* www.spotteddog.org

*Avuncular, kindly and well-liked by the American public, Thomas Lipton was Great Britain's unofficial ambassador of good will.* www.reprotableaux.com

he rose to fame and fortune through honest work, never forgot his roots, and was a man of outstanding character and regular habits who didn't smoke, drink or tell off-color jokes. He had two qualities cherished by the members of the NYYC. He was a keen competitor and a gracious loser.

Lipton admitted he was no yachtsman, but he had acquired a deep affection for American workers at an early age, when he spent a few years in the United States working as a common laborer. He was upset by Dunraven's behavior and wanted to restore good relations between the two countries.

When the challenge was received it took less than twenty-four hours to agree to terms. The conditions were similar to the Dunraven series. Lipton's vessel would be a cutter with a load waterline of 89.5 feet. Designed by William Fife, Jr., it would be built on the Thames River near London. Her underbody plating would be manganese bronze, her topside aluminum alloy over steel frames. Named the *Shamrock*, she would be finished and launched the following summer (June 24) and the races would be held in October of 1899.

When Sir* Thomas arrived in New York the following summer, the press emphasized his Horatio Alger-like rise to wealth and success. Americans took him to heart, considering him more "American" than the majority of the New York City Yacht Club membership.

Defending the Cup was a new boat designed by Herreshoff, the *Columbia*, bankrolled by a syndicate of some of the wealthiest men in the world — J. Pierpont Morgan, Edwin D. Morgan

---

\* His knighthood came after he made a generous donation to a royal charity during Queen Victoria's Jubilee Year.

*The* Shamrock, *right, appears to be ahead of the* Columbia, *probably taken during the third race.* Library of Congress.

and C. Oliver Iselin. J.P Morgan, commodore of the NYYC, had recently donated $200,000 worth of property on West 44th Street in Manhattan on which to build a new clubhouse. Iselin was designated the managing owner of the yacht.

Created at a cost of $250,000 (Lipton spent twice that amount), the *Columbia* was built in secrecy. She was plated with bronze over nickle-steel frames. Her master was Capt. Charles Barr and she carried a crew from Deer Isle, Maine. J.P. Morgan, at his own expense, rebuilt the *Defender* to run trials against the defender. The *Columbia* proved herself superior to the former Cup winner.

For the first time, the U.S. government managed crowd control for the races. Through an act of Congress, six revenue cutters, six torpedo boats, six tugboats (for the press) two steam yachts and a naval militia yacht made sure there was no overcrowding.

*One of the risks of crowding too much sail on a lightweight vessel is that the mast will reach the point where it gives in to the force of the wind. In this photo, taken on August 2, 1899, the* Columbia *has suffered exactly that fate.* www.jsjohnston.org

After waiting thirteen days for bad weather to clear, the first race was held on October 16. The *Columbia* won by ten minutes, eight seconds corrected time.

During the second race, the defender was leading when the challenger lost her topmast and withdrew. The *Columbia* finished the course alone, winning.

Held in a strong wind, the third race was neck-and-neck until the first mark. The defender then eased ahead and finished ahead by six minutes, thirty-four seconds, to hold the Cup.

Lipton accepted defeat graciously. He was the center of attention in a city he had loved since the age of fifteen. Now, at forty-nine, he re-established pleasant relations in the yachting world between England and the United States. His U.S. tea sales soared. To general applause, he announced, *of course* he would try again.

The *Shamrock* returned to Britain in the autumn of 1899, towed by Lipton's steam yacht, *Erin*. She was subsequently refitted by Sir Thomas and used to test the later challengers, *Shamrock II, Shamrock III*, and *Shamrock IV*.

The *Columbia* defends again in the next chapter.

# 12

# "SIR TEA" TRIES AGAIN

Lipton challenged again on October 2, 1900 and proposed
the races be held the following August under the same
conditions as the first match. He ordered a new yacht,
the *Shamrock II*, from George Watson, who had designed the
*Thistle* and both *Valkyries*. Defending the Cup was down to two
contenders, the proven *Columbia*, and a new Herreshoff design,
the *Constitution.*

Meanwhile, in Boston, a figurative storm brewed, coloring
the 1901 Cup races, although it had no effect on the actual competition. Thomas W. Lawson, a stock broker who made and lost
several fortunes, commissioned a yacht from a Boston designer,
the *Independence*, and announced his plans to enter her in the trial
races for the Cup. As he was not a member of the NYYC, the club
informed him he would have to either become a member or lend
his boat to a member. Lawson refused. A lengthy correspondence

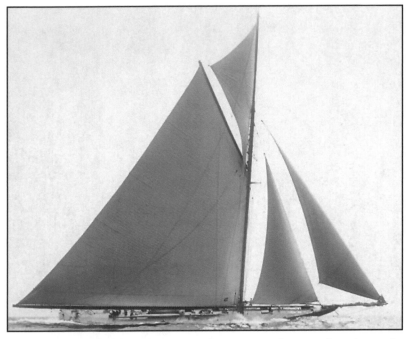

*While she looks slick and seems to be moving along in this photo, the* Independence *was difficult to steer, leaked badly, and carried tons of seeped-in water.* Library of Congress.

ensued. Finally, with public opinion heavily on his side, Lawson was allowed to informally race the two contenders vying to be named Cup defender.

Unfortunately, for Lawson at least, his *Independence* was a "scow." Measuring 140 feet in length. She had a flat body, a monstrous sail spread, a deep fin keel, and was nearly impossible to steer. The first of these races was held on July 6. Lawson's boat was so slow the race committee quit timing her after the first mark. By the time she crossed the finish line, after dark, the committee had already packed up and gone home.

In the second such race Lawson's yacht came in more than an hour behind the winner. She lost two more races before being laid up for repairs. She was leaking badly and carried several tons of water. The repairs helped little. She was still difficult to steer

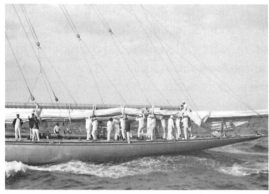

*Crew photo of the* Shamrock II, *preparing for the Cup races. www. ebay.com*

and "her bow took one angle of heel while her stern took another, through weakness of construction."

In the end Lawson's foray into America's Cup racing drew a lot more public attention than it deserved.

When a final series of three trial races was held to determine which boat would represent the NYYC, the *Columbia* was selected.

*The* Shamrock II *leads the* Columbia *across the finish line on October 3, 1901. The challenger lost the race on corrected time.* Rosenfeld Collection.

The *Shamrock II* was the first Cup challenger designed through tank testing. Her designer tested eleven different paraffin models and sixty different modifications over a nine-month period. The result looked nearly the same as other bronze-hulled boats, and once launched, she had a hard time beating the original *Shamrock* around the course.

The challenger and defender met for the first race on September 28, 1901. The *Shamrock II* took the lead off the starting line, but the *Columbia* eventually passed her, winning by one minute twenty seconds corrected time. In the next race the challenger was ahead when the race was cancelled due to lack of wind. The second complete race was again won by the defender in three minutes thirty-five seconds corrected time. The third race was the closest ever in Cup competition, with the challenger crossing the finish line two seconds ahead of the defender, but losing on time allowance by forty-one seconds.

Lipton expressed sharp disappointment, saying that Watson had done a fine job, but Herreshoff's design was better. Many Americans shared his disappointment, but took heart when he cheerfully promised to return.

The *Shamrock II* was laid up in Erie Basin for the winter.

# 13

# A SHAMROCK
# HAS THREE LEAVES

While Sir Thomas entered his first America's Cup challenge as a lark, with the added advantage of boosting tea sales in the United States, he now had racing fever and was out to win. He offered to challenge again in 1902. The NYYC turned him down, based on the section of the new Deed of Gift that prevented a challenger from returning until two years had elapsed or another challenge had taken place.

He then challenged for the summer of 1903. Conditions were amicably and quickly arrived at.

By now the focus of the America's Cup race had greatly changed. In the beginning the Cup itself was an award to the fastest yacht in a sportsmanlike race or series of races. Although it symbolized the fastest sailing yacht in the world, the race was what mattered, the trophy was secondary. As the first decade of the new century began, the focus shifted to the trophy itself.

*The differences and similarities can be seen in the drydock photos of the* Shamrock III, *above, and the* Reliance, *below. Top,* forum.woodenboat.com, *bottom,* Library of Congress.

Acquiring the trophy became the end all and be all of the yacht-ing world's effort. This was due to a great extent to the NYYC's seeming iron hold on it. In addition, by 1903 America's Cup racing had become a very specialized sport. A contender had to lay out a small fortune for a stripped-down new boat that would be of no use for any other purpose once the races were over, so lightly built that she seldom lasted more than one or two seasons. Only multimillionaires and eternal optimists would bother. Fortunately, Sir Thomas Lipton was both.

Lipton had commissioned a new challenger, the *Shamrock III*. She was designed by the same William Fife who created Sir Thomas' original *Shamrock*. On the other side of the Atlantic the NYYC created another syndicate (which included a Rockefeller and a Vanderbuilt) to develop a defender. The syndicate easily agreed to again turn to Herreshoff, who then created the *Reliance*.

Working under tight security as usual, Herreshoff was ex-tremely reticent. Just before the defender was launched in April he was interviewed by a Boston reporter.

"What do you think of the *Reliance*, Mr. Herreshoff?"

"I have nothing to say."

"Will she beat the *Constitution*?"

Silence.

"What is your opinion of *Shamrock III*?"

Silence.

"Good day, Mr. Herreshoff."

"Good day, sir." He walked away a pace, then turned. "Now please do not make this interview long. Do not print any more information than I have given you."

With an overall length of almost 140 feet and carrying more than 16,000 square feet of sail on her steel mast, the *Reliance* was, until then, the largest defender ever built. She was Hershoff's *Vigilant* developed to extremes. Yacht historian Winfield Thomp-son described her as "the prototype of a vicious kind of yacht,

*In this photo, the* Reliance's *more than 16,000 square feet of sail dwarf the vessel's hull.* Rosenfeld Collection.

whose existence has been more of a curse than a blessing to the sport of yacht racing."

The *Reliance* gave no compromise when it came to speed. Her hull plating was too thin, her sail area too large and her overhangs too extreme to be seaworthy. Yachting purists disliked the overhangs as they served no purpose other than to fudge the 90-foot waterline limit imposed by the Deed of Gift. In a breeze of five to seven knots she would heel over such that her waterline was extended to 130 feet, giving her more speed. One critic said she was "perhaps the most wonderful and useless racing machine known to yachting."

The *Shamrock III* was built similar to the defender, only she was slightly shorter in overall length (134 feet) and not quite as extreme. Both vessels were considered huge, lightly built skimming dishes of an extreme type that needed a crew of more than sixty to sail them. The training and experience of the captain and crew on the two vessels was quite different — the American crews were experienced and used to working together, the Irish crews were not. That, and the experience of the two captains made the difference.

The first race was held on August 22 and won by the defender in nine minutes. She also won the second race, on August 25, by three minutes and sixteen seconds. The third race was held on September 3. The *Reliance* beat the challenger to the outer mark by eleven minutes and seven seconds. As the two yachts turned

*The* Reliance *and the* Shamrock III *just before the start of the August 22, 1903 race.* www.pistonhead.com

toward the finishing line a blanket of fog blew over the course. Neither spectators, committee boat, nor the two boats could see anything. As the fog lifted the defender crossed the finish line. The *Shamrock III* was off the course to the northeast and didn't bother to finish. The race and the Cup again belonged to the NYYC.

Facing reporters afterward, Lipton seemed discouraged for the first time:

"It is the greatest disappointment of my life. What can I do. I have tried my best ... They tell me that I have a beautiful boat. I don't want a beautiful boat. What I want is a boat to lift the Cup — a *Reliance*. Give me a homely boat, the homeliest boat that was ever designed, if she be like the *Reliance*."

World War I would start and end before Sir Thomas returned, but he would return.

The *Reliance*'s career was short-lived, and she was sold for scrap in 1913.

# 14

# "AULD MUG" WITHIN REACH

Enough is enough, agreed the yachtsmen on both sides of the Atlantic. The *Reliance* and the *Shamrock III* emphasized the extremes of America's Cup yachts. This type of boat was outrageously expensive, too large, carried too much sail, was unsafe, unseaworthy and had no practical purpose beyond the one series of races for which it was designed. Something had to be done.

In New York a committee was formed to create a new set of rules that would make the *Reliance*-type yacht obsolete. In brief, the new format took into account displacement and waterline length while penalizing excessive sail area and overhangs, making the resulting craft safer and more seaworthy. Called the Universal Measurement Rule, it was adopted by the NYYC in 1903 and finalized in 1905.

On the other side of the Atlantic, the British and most European clubs adopted a different set of rules in 1906, called the International Rule of Yacht Measurement, also created to produce sounder, more seaworthy boats. But, there was one drawback. A yacht designed to race for the Cup under New York's Universal Rule could not race in Great Britain without taking heavy penalties. The International Rule would not be accepted in America until 1929.

After waiting in the hope the contradictions between the two rules would sort themselves out, Sir Thomas Lipton forwarded a challenge in 1907, agreeing to conform to the Universal Rule. He also asked the NYYC to agree the dimensions of the defender would not exceed those of the challenger.

The New York club said no. Although they had adopted the Universal Rule for their regular races, they held that the Deed of Gift governed America's Cup races and under the deed they could have a waterline length of up to 90 feet. J. Pierpont Morgan stated that the Cup should only be raced for by "the fastest and most powerful vessels that can be produced."

Five years later Sir Thomas challenged once more, specifying a boat with a 75-foot waterline. He asked that the club would promise to build a defender no larger than that. Again they refused, saying, under the deed, they could build up to 90 feet. The following year, in 1913, Lipton resubmitted his challenge, unconditionally. This time the club accepted, then, under the deed's mutual agreement clause, acknowledged it would limit its defender to a waterline of 75 feet and build it based on the Universal Rule. In other words, after a lot of posturing by the NYYC, the original challenge was accepted.

The new *Shamrock IV* was being towed across the Atlantic and had reached Bermuda when World War I broke out. She continued on to New York and was stored in drydock on arrival. It was 1920 before the match was held. The only disagreement in the final negotiations was the NYYC wanted to hold the races in the less congested waters of Newport, Rhode Island, while Lipton

SHAMROCK IV (1920)
ROYAL ULSTER YACHT CLUB
DESIGNER — C.E. NICHOLSON
L.O.A. — 110'0"
L.W.L. — 75'0"
DISPLACEMENT — 104 TONS
DRAUGHT — 13'8"
SAIL AREA — 9 860 SQUARE FEET

AMERICA'S CUP YACHT — "SHAMROCK IV"

*This detailed drawing of the* Shamrock IV *shows her from top to bottom and gives some of her specifics.* www.flickr.com.

preferred New York because of the public attention he received. In the end the club deferred to Lipton.

For the first time in America's Cup racing nearly the entire afterguard (the helmsman and his advisors) were amateurs. Charles Francis Adams of Boston (later Secretary of the Navy under Herbert Hoover) manned the defender's helm. William P. Burton, known as a brilliant tactician, steered for Lipton. This transition was smooth on the defending boat, but chaotic on the *Shamrock IV*. Burton insisted on having his wife as timekeeper,

*William P. Burton at the helm of the* Shamrock IV *during trials. Seated next to him is Charles Nicholson, the boat's designer, who would be removed from the yacht after the first race.* www. inverclyde.gov.uk

despite strong feelings among the crew about having a woman on board. The boat was stripped down (to save weight) to such a degree that there was no way to brew tea, also upsetting to the crew. In the first race Burton crossed the starting line too soon and had to go around and approach it again, a common occurrence, but embarrassing nonetheless. Finally there were too many conflicting suggestions from the afterguard during the race. This escalated to the point that Sir Thomas pulled the boat's designer, Charles Nicholson, off the yacht.

The first race was won by the *Shamrock IV* after the Herreshoff-designed *Resolute* lost a halyard and the afterguard decided to retire. This was the first time a defender failed to finish a race. They might have continued had they known the challenger was in danger of losing her mast in the stiff wind, but this was kept quiet until after the race. Ever the sportsman, Sir Thomas offered to resail the race, but the committee refused.

The second race was won by Burton and his superior seamanship in light winds. He defeated the *Resolute* by two minutes twenty-six seconds corrected time. This was the first time a challenger beat a defender in the entire history of the Cup races. Sir Thomas was overjoyed, saying he was "the happiest man in the world." The spectator fleet shared his joy. The score was now 2-0. One more win and the Cup would be his.

*The* Resolute, *left, and the* Shamrock IV *approaching the starting line at the beginning of the fifth race.* www.flysfo.com

In the third race both boats ran the course in exactly the same time, but the defender won because of her time allowance of more than six minutes.

In the fourth race, the *Resolute* won by almost ten minutes on corrected time. That made it 2-2.

Crowds of spectators came out the next two days, but there was no wind and the races were postponed. On the third day the wind came up a gale, 25-30 knots, bringing another delay.

The defender took the lead in light winds during the fifth race and won by nearly twenty minutes, corrected time. The NYYC again retained the Cup.

When reporters asked the 70-year old Lipton if he would come back, he hesitated, then said he didn't know. He did return one more time, ten years later.

In 1925 the *Resolute* was sold to E. Walter Clark of Philadelphia.

# 15

# LIPTON'S SWAN SONG

In 1927 there was a pivotal meeting of the International Yacht Racing Union and the North American Yacht Racing Union which resulted in a series of measurement rules and racing regulations designed to bring sportsmanship and uniformity to yacht racing in general and the America's Cup in particular. The item which interested Sir Thomas required large yachts to meet Lloyd's construction specifications. This meant that defenders, as well as challengers, would have to be constructed strong enough to withstand an Atlantic crossing. This took away the traditional speed advantage American boats had of being more lightly built.

Lipton challenged in May of 1929. In the ensuing negotiations he was pleasantly surprised when the NYYC suggested the boats be built under the Universal Rule, to the top rating of either the J or K class,* that the races be held without time allowances and the winner of four of seven races would take the Cup. Sir Thomas quickly agreed, choosing the J class, meaning the boat's length on the waterline would be between 75 and 87 feet. He also agreed to holding the races off Newport, Rhode Island, to get away from the spectator traffic congestion and pollution in the Sandy Hook area.

While it may sound as if the J Class was a downward trend from earlier contenders, in actuality, they were longer, heavier and far more costly. They were in every way larger than the 1920 Cup boats except in beam measurement and sail area, and, in fact, the heaviest yachts to race since 1871. What really set them apart was the sail plan. Called the Bermuda or Marconi** rig, a single, tall, triangular mainsail and large mast replaced earlier designs. Thus, the sail area was about half the expanse found in the older Cup boats and the new shape was much more efficient, producing a faster boat than the larger, earlier boats.

Lipton's boat was the *Shamrock V*, a centerboard cutter measuring 77 feet on the load waterline, designed by Charles Nicholson. She was built with steel, teak, pine, mahogany, elm and spruce, carried 78 tons of lead in her keel, and was considered the finest looking *Shamrock* of all.

The NYYC created two syndicates for the defense and encouraged others as well. The result was four potential defenders: the *Enterprise*, designed by W. Starling Burgess, the *Whirlwind* designed by L. Francis Herreshoff, the *Yankee* designed by Frank Paine, and the *Weetamoe* designed by Clinton Crane. The four boats cost a total of $3,000,000, with the *Enterprise* alone costing almost $1 million (and this during the Depression).

---

* The Universal Rule rates two-masted racers as classes A through H and single-masted racers as classes I through S. In the late 1920s the trend was towards smaller, safer boats, hence the J or K class.

** It was called the Marconi Rig because the tall mast, heavily stayed at the sides, resembled the towers and guy lines on Marconi wireless stations that were common at the time.

*The* Shamrock V *was considered the best looking of all the yachts to carry that name.* Beken & Son.

Harold Vanderbilt was captain and manager of the *Enterprise*. A man with an orderly and inventive mind, he made his own rules. He developed a mathematical formula to define the helmsman's job in arriving at the starting line just as the gun went off. He organized his crew like a machine. Each man was given a number according to his assignment and given a jersey with the number printed on it. When orders were given, numbers, not names, were called out. The afterguard was assigned special tasks. Vanderbilt steered at starts and upwind while someone else steered downwind. His sail-trimmer steered when the wind was light or when Vanderbilt needed a break to calm his nerves.

*Harold S. Vanderbilt was competitive, efficient, well-organized, yet compassionate.* Rosenfeld Collection.

Burgess developed his design for the *Enterprise* by towing models through a test tank, testing sails in a wind tunnel and doing structural tests at the Bureau of Standards. Before deciding on the boat's length, he checked records of wind velocities off Newport in September for the previous twenty years. When the yacht was completed she was full of gadgets, inventions and exotic new materials. She had two centerboards, for sailing on and off the wind, and her stripped-down hull held some twenty-four winches below decks. She had a shunt dynamometer to measure strain on the headstays and backstays, a strain gauge to measure the degree of compression on the leeward side of the mast.

*The interior of the* Enterprise *was stripped of everything not essential (including the toilet). The interior winches can be seen at left.* Rosenfeld Collection.

LIPTON'S SWAN SONG **85**

*The Enterprise's hollow duralumin mast was 152 feet tall and held together with 80,000 rivets.* Richard V. Simpson.

One thing she didn't have was a toilet. Any item that didn't directly add to the boat's ability to win was done away with. The crew had to manage as best they could.

A major innovation was her mast. Made of duralumin, it was lighter than standard wood masts by about a ton, giving her a major advantage in stability. Another was her boom. Named the "Park Avenue" it was four feet wide, enough for two men to walk its length side by side, and fitted with transverse slides so

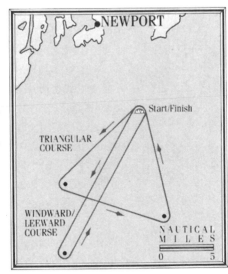

*The J-Class courses were run on either a windward/leeward or triangular course off Newport, Rhode Island. Each was about thirty miles in distance.* Sail Magazine.

Two seamen inspecting the far end of the Enterprise's 66½-foot "Park Avenue" boom. Stanley Rosenfeld.

the foot of the sail could slide from side to side, assuming its natural aerodynamic shape on either tack. Traditional yachtsmen called her "a mechanical yacht" and a "box of clockwork." On August 27 the *Enterprise* was selected as defender.

In the end the *Shamrock V* was no match for the defender. She was poorly rigged and badly handled. She lost the first race by two minutes and fifty-two seconds and the second by nine minutes and thirty-four seconds. In the third race her main halyard parted and the mainsail fell. She was towed back to her dock and Vanderbilt sailed the course alone and claimed victory. In the fourth race the *Enterprise* easily sailed to a nine minute, ten second lead at the weather mark, coasted the two final legs on reduced sail and won by five minutes and forty-four seconds.

*Solomon Islands commemorative stamp of the winning* Enterprise. *Philatelic International.*

It was a sad victory. Lipton tried so hard for so long and was such a good sport. He was eighty years old and in failing health. As he neared the finish of the race, Vanderbilt wrote in is diary, "Our hour of triumph, our hour of victory, is all but at hand but it is so tempered with sadness that it is almost hollow."

Will Rogers suggested that everyone send a dollar to a Lipton Cup Fund, c/o New York's Mayor Walker, to buy Sir Thomas a consolation cup. Within a week $16,000 dollars came in and Tiffany's produced a magnificent 18-carat gold cup. When Lipton picked it up in November, he was sincerely moved and promised to try again. Sadly, he died suddenly within a year.

Alfred Loomis best summed up Sir Thomas Lipton's impact on the America's Cup:

> The amiable tea-vending Sir Thomas Lipton bridged a generation in which American sportsmanship reached maturity and wondered why it had been such a nauseating infant ... He helped us lift Cup racing from the level of a barroom brawl and establish it as a contest between architects, legislators and sportsman-sailors.

The *Shamrock V* was sold to Sir Thomas Sopwith in 1931. She was later sold to Sir Richard Fairey who incorporated aerodynamic and hydrodynamic modifications and raced her against other J-Class yachts during the 1935 regatta season. In 1937 she was sold to Mario Crespi and renamed *Quadrifoglio* (cloverleaf). Crespi also modified her for interior comfort. In 1962 she was sold to Italian yachtsman Piero Scanu who spent three years overhauling her in England and reverted to her original name. In 1986 *Shamrock V* was returned to the Lipton Tea Company who donated her to the Museum of Yachting at Newport, Rhode Island. Following changes of ownership in the 1990s she took part in the America's Cup Jubilee in the Solent in 2001.

# 16

# A NEAR THING

Thomas Octave Murdoch (T.O.M.) Sopwith challenged for the Cup in 1933 through the Royal Yacht Squadron. His talent for attracting attention in American waters began in 1912 when he fell in the ocean off Coney Island while barnstorming as a stunt flyer. He also made news when he buzzed the statue of William Penn on the top of City Hall in Philadelphia. He later raced motor boats and made a fortune building Sopwith Camel warplanes for Great Britain during World War I. Throwing himself into sailing, he won the 12-Meter Championships every year from 1927 to 1930.

Following negotiations, the terms for the next Cup were announced in February of 1934. The match would be a four-out-of-seven series held off Newport, Rhode Island. For the first time, the NYYC would allow the challenging club to substitute another boat if Sopwith's boat wasn't satisfactory. Below-deck

*Thomas Sopwith with a determined look on his face poses at the helm. His wife, Phyllis, appearing equally determined, was part of the afterguard in his races. Rosenfeld Collection.*

winches would be prohibited, heavier masts were required, and each competing yacht would have to include living quarters for the crew.

The new terms put the *Enterprise* out of business. She was given to a junk dealer on consignment and her duralumin mast ended up as part of the radio tower at the Rhode Island State Police barracks.

With the experience gained on his recently acquired *Shamrock V*, Sopwith went to her designer, Charles Nicholson for a new boat. The result was the *Endeavour*, a centerboarder with a waterline length of 83 feet, a steel hull and a steel mast.

Just before leaving for the United States, the crew of the challenger went on strike for higher wages. Sopwith fired most of them, hiring amateurs as replacements. It would be a costly decision, for although the replacements were experienced, they had not trained together, were timid and comparatively slow.

Defending the Cup was the *Rainbow*, closely resembling the challenger in size and general appearance. She was designed by Starling Burgess. Mike Vanderbilt was her skipper and manager. With the Great Depression still on everyone's mind, it was emphasized that the yacht only cost $400,000. Much of the equipment from the *Enterprise* was used and some of the sails were borrowed from other boats. This was all in the interest of public relations, for the *Rainbow* syndicate included four Vanderbilts, J.P. Morgan and several other wealthy backers.

The *Rainbow* fought an uphill battle to become defender. Facing the *Weetamoe* and *Yankee*, both revamped to meet the new rules, she consistently lost to the latter vessel. But Vanderbilt and Burgess fiddled with the location of the ballast and tried different sails. They also rigged a flexible boom that shaped the sail better than the Park Avenue boom, and made other improvements. Soon she was winning the trials. In the end the *Rainbow* was selected, not because she was faster, but because Vanderbilt was a better sailor and manager.

Before the first race of the match, Sopwith filed a protest. Maintaining the *Rainbow* had not followed the spirit of the new regulations, he objected to her stripped out interior. The race committee examined the two yachts and agreed. The solution was to allow Sopwith to remove furniture and fittings from his vessel, including his bathtub.

As the two boats prepared for the first race on September 17, the *Endeavour* had a hard time getting her mainsail up in rough seas. The NYYC race committee, without authorization and

*The* Endeavour, *leading, with the* Rainbow, *approaching the starting line during one of the 1934 races.* Rosenfeld Collection.

contrary to the conditions of the match, granted a fifteen-minute postponement to let the challenger get properly prepared.

As it was, the two boats crossed the starting line a second apart. The *Endeavour* was ahead when the defender's inner spinnaker boom lift parted, sending the spinnaker pole crashing to the deck. It took a minute to repair and Sopwith crossed the finish line two minutes and nine seconds ahead, winning the first race.

In the second race, the following day, Sopwith was ahead at the start and stayed there. He won the second race by fifty-one seconds. At that point, in betting circles, he became the two-to-one favorite to win the Cup.

The NYYC and Mike Vanderbilt began to get nervous. In the third race with Vanderbilt at the helm, Sopwith was six minutes, twenty-one seconds ahead at the final mark. It looked so hopeless that Vanderbilt turned the wheel over to Sherman Hoyt, his relief helmsman and a wily tactician. Hoyt noticed that Sopwith constantly tried to keep the defender covered, regardless of where

*The* Rainbow *with her lee rail dipping under during one of the 1934 races.*
Beken.

they were on the course. As they came down toward the finish line, Hoyt luffed past the *Endeavour*'s weather side, hoping Sopwith would follow. He did, tacking into a calm area. The *Rainbow* altered course, sailed through the challenger's wake, and continued on to the finish line, leaving the *Endeavour* three minutes, twenty-six seconds behind, tacking furiously to find the wind. Now it was two to one, in Sopwith's favor, but looking better.

The fourth race, held on September 22, brought out the first protest flag by a challenger in the history of the Cup. There were two incidents: while jockeying for position approaching the starting line there was a near collision with each skipper claim-

*Sherman Hoyt was gifted in tactics and won the day for the* Rainbow *in the third and sixth races.* Morris Rosenfeld & Sons.

ing the other was at fault, and, as the two boats rounded the first mark, the defender forced the challenger to give way and lose speed. Sopwith's protest flag did not appear until the contenders approached the committee boat near the finish line, two hours later. Vanderbilt won the race by one minute, fifteen seconds.

Sopwith thought he would win the protest, which included both incidents. The following day the race committee announced they would not consider the protest as the flag was not raised "promptly" according to the rules, but three hours after the first incident, two after the second.

There was a unanimous outcry from the press favoring Sopwith which caused the committee to explain its reasoning. The first incident had occurred in full view of the committee boat, all saw it, and Sopwith should have been disqualified, making the second incident moot. Regardless, they allowed the race to continue in the interest of sportsmanship.

Vanderbilt went on to win the fifth race from a morose Sopwith by four minutes, four seconds.

The sixth race was strangely similar to the third. Sopwith was well in the lead, the helm of the *Rainbow* was turned over to Hoyt, he again gambled on Sopwith following him away from the finish line, which he did, and Hoyt turned for the line, coming in fifty-five seconds ahead of the challenger.

The Cup remained in New York.

# 17

# THE UNBEATABLE RANGER

Sopwith challenged again in 1936 through the Royal Yacht Squadron. In accepting, the NYYC agreed to let him enter the *Endeavor* again if his new boat, the *Endeavor II* did not come up to expectations. The races were scheduled for July and August 1937, under the same rules as the previous match.

It was obvious a new defender was needed. Unfortunately The Great Depression was at its zenith and money was scarce, even among the members of the NYYC. However, once the designers agreed to reduce their fees and the Bath Iron Works offered to build the boat at cost, Mike Vanderbilt offered to pay all the expenses. He summed up the situation in a poem, published in the July 1937 issue of *Redbook* magazine:

> My mast is duralumin, but it's costlier than gilt,
> The wind that fills my riggin' is a million dollar breeze.

*The* Endeavour II *stretching her legs before the 1937 races.* www.corbisimages. com

From my bowsprit to my topsail, I am wholly Vander-built
And I only go a-sailing in the most exclusive seas.

The nations mourn the income tax, for bread the countries cry.
But whistle the *Endeavour* out, and run the pennants up —
Three quarter million dollars will be racing in July
For a mid-Victorian trophy, for a silver-plated cup.

His poem says as much about himself and his position in the higher financial strata of society as it does about the race for the Cup.

Vanderbilt brought in two designers, Starling Burgess and Olin Stephens. They each made two models and all four were tested in the tank at the Stevens Institute. According to Stephens, the final design was one of Burgess'.

Given the name *Ranger*, the new boat was built to the maximum J-class waterline of 87 feet. She was huge, powerful, made

*According to Vanderbilt his* Ranger *was "the fastest all-around sailing vessel that has ever been built." She proved her worth in the 1937 Cup races.* Rosenfeld Collection.

of welded steel and included many advances. However, traditional yachtsmen considered her not a very pretty boat. She was blunt at the bow, flat in the stern and carried a formidable amount of canvas, including an 18,000 square foot spinnaker, greater than the total sail area of most previous Cup contenders.

While being towed around Cape Cod from the Bath yard to New York she hit rough weather and lost her mast and most

*The* Ranger's *afterguard included the "braintrust" above, left to right, Roderick Stephens, Olin Stephens, Prof. Zenas Bliss, Mr. & Mrs. Harold Vanderbilt and Arthur Knapp. Vanderbilt's ability to assemble the right team and hard work were the keys to his success.* Rosenfeld Collection.

*Crew accommodations aboard the* Ranger *as viewed from the owner's stateroom.* Rosenfeld Collection.

of her rigging. The trial races were less than two weeks away. The owners of the *Yankee* and the *Rainbow*, both of which the *Ranger* was scheduled to compete against in the trials, offered whatever spare equipment they had and voluntarily postponed the preliminary races by four days. With their help repairs were quickly made.

The *Ranger* beat the others in four races, won all the observation trial matches, and was chosen after just one race against the *Yankee*. She was poised for greatness.

In the Cup match, the *Endeavour II* lost the first race by seventeen minutes. She did worse in the second race. At this point Sopwith had her hauled out to examine the bottom. There was fear that she was performing poorly because she somehow snagged a lobster pot, or some such, on her keel, slowing her down. The bottom was clean, she was put back in the water, and lost the next two races.

The *Ranger* was truly unbeatable.

The NYYC was relieved when Sopwith pronounced it a fair contest and had no complaints.

In his book, *On the Wind's Highway*, Vanderbilt waxed a bit lyrical about the J-boats racing that season: "As they have come out of the distance, so they shall go into the distance. The fair wind, their never weary white wings, carry them on — On the Wind's Highway, 'homeward bound for orders' — on, to destiny."

Ironically, with World War II approaching, the boats were scrapped, melted down and became parts of tanks, guns and bullets. It would be twenty-one years before the next America's Cup match. And that would be with an entirely new type of boat.

# 18

# THE
# 12-METER BOAT
# VS. THE CUP

After World War II nobody seemed interested in the
America's Cup. Yachtsmen everywhere were apathetic.
In 1948 the commodore of the NYYC and the commodore of the Royal Ocean Racing Club of England met to dis-
cuss how to generate interest. They agreed that a good beginning
would be to make ocean-racing yachts smaller (and more affordable), measuring about 45 feet on the waterline. Their proposal
was rejected by the membership of the NYYC.

By the 1950s the lack of interest and lack of a challenger
forced the NYYC to the point where it had to decide either to put
the Cup on permanent display as a piece of history or modify the
Deed of Gift in some way to encourage competition. Fortunately
for the history of the America's Cup they chose the later. This was
due, in a great part, to the persuasiveness and negotiating skills
of Commodore Henry Sears.

## WHAT IS A 12-METER BOAT?

The term "12-Meter" is not based on any single measurement. It is the result of a formula that governs design and construction. Typically 12-Meter Class boats are sloop-rigged, with masts roughly 85 feet tall. Competitiveness is maintained by requiring the boats conform to the 12-Meter formula. Designers are free to change any of the variables in the formula as long as the final result is 12 meters or less and the boat is both seaworthy and safe. The formula creates similarity in boat design while allowing enough variation so that races are as much about design and construction as they are about seamanship and tactics. The formula used in 1958* was:

$$\frac{L + 2d + \sqrt{S} - F}{2.37} \leq 12 \text{ meters}$$

L = waterline length
d = difference between skin girth and chain girth**
S = sail area
F = freeboard

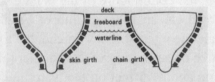

---

\*     In later years the formula was adjusted to conform to advances in materials and technology.

**    Skin girth is the length of an imaginary line drawn at the widest breadth from one side, downward along the hull surface, to the keel and up to the other side. Chain girth is measured the same, but as if a chain were being used, thus the measurement does not conform to concave areas of the hull.

The deed was amended and signed on December 17, 1956. The new standard for the America's Cup would be a 12-meter boat based on the International Rule developed in Europe. The minimum waterline length was changed to 44 feet. The NYYC racing rules were replaced with internationally agreed racing rules. And, challengers no longer had to sail to the contest. Their yacht could arrive aboard a freighter, or by other means.

Before six months had gone by, the Royal Yacht Squadron issued a challenge for a match in 1958. This produced a whirlwind of activity on both sides of the Atlantic.

In England the first 12-meter boat was built in 1907, a year after the adoption of the International Rule. Roughly 100 were subsequently built, with about half still afloat, but none had been built since World War II. A syndicate was formed to create a boat for the coming match. It included two "Sirs," two Lords, one Lt. Col., one Major, one Group Captain, and several others. A yachting writer described them as: "…a group of kindly, elegant, elderly British gentry, whose sense of loyalty and gallantry was infinitely superior to their sense of competition and their critical understanding of boat speed."

The syndicate asked four of England's best designers to create models for tank tests. A total of eight models were towed in the Saunders-Roe Experimental Tank. After forty-one hours of testing, the model created by Scotsman David Boyd was chosen as being the fastest. The new boat would be named *Sceptre*.

Their selection method had several hidden problems. All the models were designed for a brisk breeze, which may or may not be encountered off Newport, the site of the matches. The test tank had no wave-making machine, so the models were towed under unrealistic conditions simulating a strong wind and flat water. The model chosen had rounded forward sections — the worst possible hull design for the confused, choppy seas normally encountered in these races.

Back in New York, Commodore Henry Sears put all his persuasive skills to work convincing a reluctant group and finally brought together a worthwhile syndicate which included Briggs Cunningham, Gerald Lambert and Vincent Astor. They commissioned Olin Stephen to design a new 12-meter yacht, to be named *Columbia*.

Soon interest, and even enthusiasm, came from other quarters. Chandley Hovey, a retired stockbroker in Boston built a 12-meter boat, the *Easterner*, for the trials to select a defender. Henry Marcer, a retired shipping executive and member of the NYYC (but not the syndicate), commissioned the *Weatherly*. John Matthews, also a shipping executive, entered the *Vim*, built in 1939 for Harold Vanderbilt (Mike's son), and a successful racer in his own right.

In the first trials the *Weatherly* and the *Easterner* were eliminated. This left the *Vim* and the *Columbia* vying to be named defender. At first the 19-year old *Vim* won every race. In fact, the *Columbia* was the faster boat and she proved it, once the crew gained experience working together, and won four of the last six races. The *Columbia* was chosen as defender.

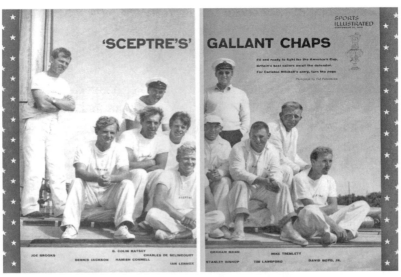

Sports Illustrated *did a two page spread showing the Sceptre's "under 30-years of age" crew.* yachtingclassics.blogspot.com

Across the Atlantic, the *Scep-tre*'s preparations continued downhill. Her syndicate decided that none of the deck crew would be over 30, automatically eliminating anyone with experience in 12-meter boats. Her final crew was chosen on June 23, leaving little time for training or fine-tuning the boat. She trained against the *Evaine*, a prewar 12-meter badly beaten by the *Vim*. She could barely beat the *Evaine*.

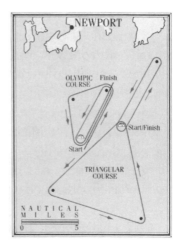

The first race was held on September 20, 1958. Within fifteen minutes is was clear the *Sceptre* was no competition. The defender won

*In 1958 the competitors sailed either around a triangular course or a windward/leeward course. Each course was about 24 miles long. Sail Magazine.*

*The* Columbia, *left, leading the* Sceptre, *as she did in all four races.*
stephenlirakis.blogspot.com

four straight races by margins of from seven to fifteen minutes.

President Eisenhower watched the first race from a destroyer and left before it ended for a round of golf. The *New York Herald Tribune* commented on the last race, "It is a spectacle calculated to make the tea break at a cricket test seem wildly exciting."

At the final press conference, the chairman of the British syndicate, Hugh Goodman, said "We are very glad the America's Cup has ended on a happy note for everyone but us."

At least the series ended without controversy and good sportsmanship prevailed.

The challenger is now owned and sailed in British waters by the *Sceptre* Preservation Society.

The winner went on to a long career as a competitor in the defender trials for the 1962, 1964, and 1967 America's Cup competitions.

# 19

# THUNDER FROM DOWN UNDER

In October 1959 the Royal Sydney Yacht Squadron announced its intention of challenging for the America's Cup in 1962, to be brought by publishing tycoon Frank Packer. If the English were aware of this, they ignored it. A member of the Royal Thames Yacht Club was on his way to New York to present their challenge for 1962 when Packer heard about it. He cabled a formal challenge ahead which was immediately accepted by the NYYC. The English, thinking that they had exclusivity when it came to challenges, were outraged.

For several months telegrams flew between London, New York and Sydney. The British tried to get the Aussies to withdraw. When this failed, they tried to convince them to agree to a Commonwealth challenge, with the winner moving on to the Cup match. Packer told them, "Maybe we won't do any better, but every now and again you have to give the young fellow in the family his head."

In May 1960 Mill Northan, a member of the Sydney syndicate, happened to be in London and was invited to attend a Royal Thames Yacht Club meeting. In a letter to Packer, he described the event:

> I walked into the room and there were twenty blokes, mostly Lords and Earls, and at the head of the table the old cobber the Duke [of Edinburgh]. I don't mind telling you I started to feel nervous, as nobody told me he was to be present. However, he left his chair despite the stony stares at me and walked over and shook me by the hand and said he was glad I could attend and I sat down at the opposite end of the large table like a shag on a rock, facing HRH [His Royal Highness] at the other end.
>
> The meeting opened as per the agenda enclosed and for a long time I looked at a lot of necks, nobody even troubling to look my way, and I chipped in when HRH asked me whether we had changed our minds with regard to elimination tests and I swear you could have heard a pin drop when I took it upon myself to say NO and believe me he really grinned and asked why not. I explained that it was in my opinion too late to alter. Owen Aisher (a big shot) and Lord Craigmyle surprised me by saying 'hear, hear.' Then we got cracking.
>
> He directed more questions at me than anyone in the room and I swear that at the finish I had 95 percent on our side and it was unanimous that Australia was the logical challenger and we had all their good wishes and definite offers to help ... Apparently I saved a sticky meeting and we all had lunch and a few snorts and everyone was happy and I finished up in a corner with HRH and we had a long friendly yarn.

Frank Packer, owner of the Australian Consolidated Press, enjoyed keeping people on their toes. With a reputation for whimsically firing his editors, his publishing empire was known, behind his back, as "Packerstan." When asked what inspired his Cup challenge, his reply was, "Alcohol and delusions of grandeur."

His battle plan for the Cup began with the hiring of Alan Payne, Australia's only professional naval architect, to design his boat. He then chartered the *Vim* for four years as a training platform for his crew and for Payne as an example of the type of boat he expected.

*Sir Frank Packer was not a person to be taken lightly.* www.groupbuyit.ca

Payne, in turn, convinced the NYYC to let him use the Stevens Institute to test his hull models. He then got permission to use American-made sailcloth, winches, mast extrusions and a boom. His creation, built in secrecy, was revealed on February 28. She was named *Gretel* after Mr. Packer's deceased wife.

Meanwhile, in New York, the NYYC prepared for trial races to determine which boat would be the defender. The *Columbia* reappeared. She was bought for $150,000 in 1960 by the Shields family. Henry Mercer rebuilt the *Weatherly*. The *Easterner*, from Boston, was hopeful. A new yacht of radical design, the *Nefertiti*, was built.

After six races the *Easterner* and the *Columbia* were eliminated. The *Nefertiti*, which was a fair competitor in heavy weather, but slow in light winds, lost four out of five races to the *Weatherly*, which became the defender.

When the Aussies arrived in Newport in 1962, they turned the town upsidedown. Viewed by many as crashing an exclusive, established traditional venue, all they wanted to do was make friends, hoist a few beers, get on with the races, win the Cup, and take it back to Sydney.

As the day for the first race approached, Packer began stirring things up. He put his crew through tiring drills, including testing some eighty-five sails. He refused to name his skipper until the

*The crew of the* Weatherly *working hard to offset her hard tilt to port. www.* afyacht.com

*President Kennedy and the First Lady watching the 1962 races from the deck of a destroyer.* chevaliertaglang.blogspot.com

last minute, leaving them no time to train together. On the morning of the first race he replaced his navigator with someone who wasn't familiar with Newport waters.

The first race on Saturday, was delayed by crowding due to the estimated 2,500 spectator boats clamoring for a good view. When it was over the *Weatherly*, under Bus Mosbacher, had won by three minutes, forty-three seconds.

Packer immediately booted the navigator off his boat and replaced him with an assistant helmsman.

The second race started with the defender in the lead, but on a downwind leg under spinnakers in a 25-knot wind, the challenger caught a large series of rollers that surfed her into the lead. She raced past the *Weatherly* as if she were standing still. Almost at the same moment the defender's afterguy parted and the *Gretel* won the race by forty-seven seconds.

It was the first win by a challenger since 1934. The Aussies and dozens of newfound friends celebrated in a waterfront bar

*The* Gretel, *right, sails past the* Weatherly *to win the second race.* Sail Magazine.

until dawn in one of the most boisterous celebrations ever seen in staid, old, Newport.

Sadly, although no one knew it, it was all but over. The *Weatherly* won the next three races and the NYYC, once again, retained the Cup.

Afterward Frank Packer said the races were well run and eminently fair. "We weren't beaten by the conditions. The Americans were just too good for us."

The Aussies would return.

# 20

# THE BEST TRADITION ...

Following the 1962 match the Royal Thames Yacht Club cabled a formal challenge to the NYYC. New York, deciding a rest was needed, said no. After some lengthy, heated discussions a challenge was accepted in 1964.

Organizing the attempt for the British was Anthony Boyden, a 35-year-old business tycoon and experienced 12-meter man. Boyden went to David Boyd, designer of the ill-fated *Sceptre*, for a new boat, in the theory that he learned from his previous mistakes. One thing David Boyd learned was to do his tank testing in the United States. He had the good fortune to arrive just before the NYYC issued a resolution banning challengers from using American equipment or facilities. From his experiments at the Stevens Institute, he had the bad fortune to design the *Sovereign*, a weak improvement on the *Sceptre*.

*A very nice drawing of the* Constellation, *showing her hull form, rigging and sails.* www.encore-editions.com

A search for a running mate, a vessel to compete with and work against, languished to the point that the *London Times* said it would be little short of a national disgrace if no one came forward. Finally two Australian sheep farmers, Frank and John Livingstone, agreed to finance a trial mate. Unfortunately, time was running out and the best they could do was a duplicate of the *Sceptre*, from the same yard that built the original. Named *Kurrewa V*, she was

*The* Sovereign, *making her best effort.* www.afyacht.com

*The* Constellation*'s winning crew.* www.1stdibs.com

managed by Owen Aisher who announced the two boats would compete off Newport, with the winner becoming the challenger. The *Sovereign* won, but by a slim margin.

On the other side of the Atlantic, two new boats were crafted; the *American Eagle* and the *Constellation*. Head of the syndicate commissioning the former boat was Pierre S. Du Pont III, of the chemical fortune. The syndicate responsible for the later boat was lead by Eric Ridder, a successful publisher, and Walter Gubelmann, whose fortune came from office machines.

Also in the trial mix were the *Nefertiti,* the *Easterner* and the *Columbia.* From the start the real contest was between the two new boats, the *American Eagle* and the *Constellation.* Although Ridder was skipper of the *Constellation* in title, he deferred to Bob Bavier, a writer, editor and expert sailor, to be skipper in running the boat.

The *American Eagle*'s skipper was Bill Cox, an excellent manager, but Bavier was thought the better tactician. Following

*The dejected* Sovereign *crew, presumably after the last race.* forums.
sailinganarchy.com

a difficult series of trial races, the *Constellation* was chosen to
defend the Cup.

The match was held on the Olympic course for the first
time. Its triangular 24-mile scope, the same distance as the old
windward-leeward courses, had six legs which required more
skill and tactics and made for more exciting races.

The series was a rout. The American boat won in four straight
races with times of five minutes, thirty-four seconds; twenty minutes, twenty-four seconds; six minutes, thirty-three seconds and
fifteen minutes, forty seconds. The *Sovereign*'s sum performance
was twice as bad as the *Sceptre*'s in 1958.

Yachting commentator Norris Hoyt politely said: "The challenge was in the best tradition of the empire, and it lost against modern management."

Meanwhile the Aussies were again in the offing.

# 21

# THE BEST OF THE BEST

Realizing they were too generous with the Australians in their earlier challenge (almost beaten by a hull designed in an American tank, with American sails and American extrusions) the NYYC modified the Deed of Gift shortly after the 1962 races. In the future, challengers and defenders could only have equipment, sails and design research available in their own country. Although this may have sounded fair to all, it gave the United States an edge, because American technology was far ahead of anyone else's. In essence, the defender was almost guaranteed to have the faster boat.

Critics complained that for more than a century the NYYC had simply changed the rules whenever it felt threatened by a near loss. The club responded that it did not get any advantage by changing the rules. Their advantage came from hard work. The America's Cup was always meant to symbolize national prominence in construction, design and sailing skill. The rules weren't changed, they argued, it was just that they were too accommodating previously, the challenger took advantage, and they were not going to let that happen again. The Cup would have to be won by beating New York at its own game — but not by using its equipment, too!

Realizing that the change in the rules applied only to new boats, Frank Packer decided he would "repair" the *Gretel* and handed in a challenge as soon as the 1964 races were complete. He would have Alan Payne completely redesign the boat below the waterline while everything above the deck would remain as original (American-made sails and equipment).

At almost the same time another Australian syndicate, headed by Emil Christensen, a retired ice cream tycoon, made its own challenge through the Royal Sydney Yacht Squadron. His syndicate built the *Dame Pattie*, named after Dame Pattie Menzies, the wife of the prime minister of Australia. Included among Christensen's builders was Jan Pearce, who learned his sailmaking cutting defenders' sails in Marblehead, Massachusetts.

Came the trial races to determine the Australian challenger and Jock Sturrock who, as skipper of the *Dame Pattie,* ran a much tighter ship than Packer, took eleven of thirteen races. The *Gretel* stayed home, the *Dame Pattie* was shipped to New York.

Awaiting her was the defender, *Intrepid.* Designed by Olin Stephens, with ample time, money and encouragement, she was considered the first breakthrough design of the 12-meter era. Stephens ran thirty-five variations of his hull through tank tests, ending in a design most yacht people considered ugly. He reduced the size of the keel so there would be less wetted surface, he put the rudder far aft of the keel, and he put a flap or "trim tab" on the keel's trailing edge. This gave the boat added lift and better stability when turned to leeward. All the winches were placed below deck, both to give the helmsman better visibility and to bring the weight lower, plus allowing the boom to be lowered

*Designer Olin Stephens watching one of his models for the* Intrepid *in the towing tank at the Stephens Institute in Hoboken, New Jersey. Testing fees ran to more than $30,000. Stanley Z. Rosenfeld.*

almost to deck level. Lowering the boom gave the boat more power sailing upwind.

The *Intrepid* syndicate was organized by William Strawbridge, a wealthy yachtsman who had been involved with the *American Eagle*. It included Mike Vanderbilt, now 83, and Bus Mosbacher was made skipper. The total cost of the campaign was roughly $1 million.

Trials to determine the defender included the *American Eagle*, the *Constellation*, and the *Columbia*. The *Intrepid* won eighteen of nineteen races. Her only loss was due to a navigational error.

Since their last attempt at the Cup the Aussies had discovered the value of controversy, a tactic that would develop into an art form in future Cup matches. Mosbacher was blindsided with a protest and a newspaper article in which the designer of the *Dame*

*Syndicate Manager Bill Strawbridge, left, and Skipper Bus Mosbacher discussing ways to improve the* Intrepid*'s performance.* Stanley Z. Rosenfeld.

*Pattie* accused the American team of cheating. Mosbacher was irate. "… there wasn't a word of truth in it."

The cause was the American team's successful effort to keep the challengers from knowing how many winches they had, or noticing the lowered boom. The issue was eventually resolved (without the Australians noticing the lower boom) and everyone agreed that no one had cheated. But all pretense of "sportsmanship" seemed to end when Sturrock and Mosbacher quit speaking to each other. And the Australians achieved what they were after — attention in the press.

It was a walkover for the NYYC. The *Intrepid* won the first race on September 12, 1967 by five minutes, fifty-eight seconds, and the next three races by margins of better than three-and-a-half minutes. After the second race, Australian supporters in Newport began referring to the challenger as "Damn Pity."

The only real excitement occurred in the third race when a small boat blundered onto the course. A Coast Guard helicopter, trying to chase her off, sank her with the downdraft from its blades, and in the process of rescuing the survivors, caused the defender to alter her course. Of course, the *Intrepid* won anyway.

It wasn't that the challenger was such a bad boat, it was just

*This unusual overhead view shows the* Intrepid *leading the* Dame Pattie *in one of the races of the 1967 Cup match.* www.corbisimages.com

that Mosbacher and the *Intrepid* were the best skipper/boat combination ever at that point in time.

The *Dame Pattie* later underwent a major refit to provide cabins, galley and other comforts for cruising. She is now used for private charters out of Vancouver Island.

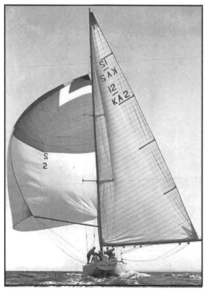

*The Australian challenger,* Dame Pattie, *was a worthwhile competitor, but easily beaten.* www.afyacht.com

*An embarrassment to the U.S. Coast Guard was their attempt to move a wayward spectator off the course in the third race. The downdraft from the helicopter rotor blades sank the spectator boat, left, and forced the* Intrepid *to alter coarse at the height of the competition. Darling.*

# 22

# LIGHTNING STRIKES
# FROM DOWN UNDER

B y 1970 it was becoming apparent that the America's Cup was not the only prize. After more than forty years in the back pages, the Cup was again front-page news. For the restless, self-made men whose egos and bank accounts required new worlds to conquer, the coming of the 12-meter era made yacht racing far more affordable. The publicity made it irresistible.

The press, hungry for oddball characters, controversy, and, if nothing else was available, some exciting races, revelled in its symbiotic relationship with wealthy yachtsmen. In 1970 that relationship was on its ascendancy.

The year 1970 saw the first formal trials to determine which country would be challenger. Sir Frank Packer returned from Australia with his new boat, the *Gretel II*.

*Baron Marcel Bich, shown here without his white gloves, arrived in Newport with Gallic flare, French wine and his own armada.* www.corbisimages.com

But the person that grabbed everyone's attention was Baron Marcel Bich, a former housewares salesman who made a fortune with his 19-cent Bic ballpoint pen. Once his wealth was in hand, he bought a title and took up yachting. He then purchased the *Kurrewa V*, his first 12-meter. She was quickly followed with the *Sovereign* and the *Constellation*. He then commissioned one of the designers of the *Nefertiti* to create a fast 12-meter. Finally he approached the challenge with the *France*, a yacht drawn in Switzerland which included all the newest elements of American design.

Baron Bich arrived in Newport like an invasion. Included was most of his armada, several support boats, some sixty sailors, two chefs and several bins of the best French wine. The cost of his assault was estimated at $4 million. And the Baron was definitely in command. He constantly changed crew rosters, tried out two helmsmen during the trials and took over the wheel himself during the fourth (and final) race. Dressed in formal white yachting togs, with white gloves, he steered into a thickening fog. When he appeared at the finish line (being towed) forty-two minutes behind the *Gretel II*, he insisted he was not lost; it was that the fog and crowding spectator boats made the conditions impossible. Accused of abandoning the race by the press, he claimed the race committee had "dishonored" him and he would never set foot or sail in Newport again.

But he would, and did.

The *Gretel II* was a new design created by Alan Payne. Even though she beat the French boat easily, he tinkered with her right up to the beginning of the Cup match.

Packer had learned a few things since his previous effort. Before leaving Australia he announced his skipper would be James "Gentleman Jim" Hardy, a winemaker by trade. He eliminated the

*This unusual photo shows the* Gretel II *from directly ahead. Notice the two steering wheels aft.* www.yachtingclassics.blog.com

tedious drills for the crew. To tune up the *Gretel II* and her crew, he chartered the *American Eagle* from Ted Turner.

Meanwhile, Olin Stephens built a new boat, larger and heavier than previous boats, with all but one winch below decks. She was named the *Valiant*. Also competing to become defender was the *Heritage*, designed, built, rigged, sailed and owned by Charley Morgan, a sailmaker and boatbuilder from St. Petersburg, Florida. Two additional boats, the *Intrepid* and the *Weatherly*, were included to create a four-boat defender's series so that two races could be held daily.

The *Intrepid* dominated the competition. She had been altered and was two

*"Gentleman Jim" Hardy skippered the* Gretel II. Stanley Rosenfeld.

*Bill "Mr. Clean" Ficker was selected to skipper the* Intrepid. *Stanley Rosenfeld.*

feet longer and heavier than she was in the previous Cup match. Syndicate manager Bill Strawbridge brought back many of her original backers, and as Bus Mosbacher was engaged elsewhere, hired William "Mr. Clean" Ficker of California as skipper.

Once the *Heritage* and the *Weatherly* were eliminated, *Intrepid* took *Valiant* by six races to one to become defender. She was the only boat since the 1901 *Columbia* to defend twice.

The complaint that fueled the first controversy, with more to come, was about a toilet. As a weight saving measure, the Americans removed the door to the defender's toilet. Frank Packer considered that a violation of the spirit and letter of the International Rule, which required minimal accommodations. Discussions followed and the door was replaced.

Then the Australians discovered the *Intrepid* had been fitted

*The* Intrepid *of 1970 was featured on this postage stamp.* Philatelic International.

with fairing sheets, made of plastic, which had the effect of extending her hull a foot or so past the rudder post. The American team argued that the waterline measurement should be taken from the rudder post forward, ignoring the fairing sheets. Packer thought they should be included. By rule, the complaint would be resolved by a member of the NYYC, who decided the fairing sheets were not part of the hull and could be left as is. This brought a letter of complaint from Packer to the NYYCs America's Cup Committee. Committee members examined the situation and ordered a slight adjustment, but otherwise left the fairing sheets as they were. Packer's livid comment was, "An Australian skipper complaining to the New York Yacht Club committee is like a man complaining to his mother-in-law about his wife."

Came the day of the first race and while maneuvering for the start, the Aussies "went hunting" for the *Intrepid*, deliberately steering a collision course, hoping to cause the defender to commit a foul. The American boat altered course twice, each time followed by the Australian boat. On the third attempt the defender held her course, forcing the challenger to veer off just before the point of collision.

Protest flags snapped upward on both boats. Then the *Gretel II* had a horrible race, getting a wrap in her spinnaker and losing a man overboard. She lost by nearly six minutes.

Afterward, in the rules room, the NYYC race committee found there was no rules violation and both protests were disallowed.

The next protest came five days later at the start of the second race. Both yachts were on the starboard tack heading toward the committee boat end of the starting line. Ficker tried to steer between the *Gretel II* and the committee boat. The Australian boat tried to close the gap. Just after the starting gun sounded the *Gretel II*'s bow hit the *Intrepid*'s port side with

*The* Intrepid, *upper left, which had the right of way, is hit on the port side by the* Gretel II. *The America's Cup committee boat is on the right.* www.sail-world.com

enough force to break off part of her bow on the *Intrepid*'s deck. Those on the committee boat saw exactly what happened. Again two protest flags shot aloft and the *Gretel II* won the race by one minute, seven seconds.

The following day the committee met. Armed with aerial photographs and the fact that most of them had actually seen what happened, they denied the Australian protest (the Australians were clearly in the wrong) and upheld the American protest. The score was now 2-0 in favor of the Americans.

Part of the problem was the Aussies simply didn't know the rules. So they studied the rule book, then ignored it and went to the press. Frank Packer, a newspaper tycoon, knew just what to do. Give a lively quote, act indignant and you get the headline, in this case *"Gretel* Robbed" appeared in an Australian paper.

The NYYC kept a dignified silence, which others took as an admission of guilt.

The general public knew only what it read in the papers: those fun-loving, homespun Aussies, the underdogs, were being railroaded by a kangaroo court created by a bunch of stuffed-shirt New York millionaire yachties.

In the third race, the American boat took the lead and kept it to win by one minute, eighteen seconds.

The *Gretel II* won the fourth race by a minute and two seconds.

In the fifth race, the *Gretel II* took a 10-length lead, but on the run to the finish the defender gained and lead the challenger across the finish line by a minute and forty-two seconds. The Cup stayed in the United States.

Part of the outfall of all the disputes in the 1970 match was the NYYC decided that from then on an international jury would hear all protests. The jury's members would not include anyone representing either the defender or the challenger. The club was taking a long step toward removing even the appearance of favoritism. The decision was a long time coming, but was it the correct move? Time would tell.

# 23

# BOND, ALAN BOND

Thanks in part to the Australians and their swashbuckling crews, worldwide interest in the America's Cup grew to the point where it equaled pre-World War II popularity. Following the 1970 competition it went beyond that with eight clubs offering challenges from five countries for the next match scheduled for 1973. Individual challenges came from Great Britain, Canada and Italy, with two from Australia and three from France.

From the beginning of the 12-meter era America's Cup campaigns became progressively more sophisticated, more technologically complex, more time-consuming and more costly. Granted, the change-over to 12-meter boats significantly reduced the cost of Cup racing, but now those dollars were much harder to find. The days when someone such as Harold Vanderbilt could finance a multi-million dollar campaign out of his personal checkbook

131

were over. Each syndicate now spent about $3 million, more than triple the costs in 1964. When this financial reality struck home, six of the eight clubs withdrew, leaving only one challenge from France and one from Australia.

Then the match was postponed to 1974 because the NYYC decided to allow aluminium-hulled boats and the syndicates needed more time to develop them.

The French challenge came again from Baron Bich. While he did a better job of controlling his temper, he still resonated with Gallic flair. First he angered everyone in France by appointing Paul Elvstrom, a Danish Olympic Champion, as helmsman and placed him in complete charge of the campaign. This led to a boat designed by a Dane, built by a Swiss, and crewed by Norwegians, Danes and Swedes. Then Elvstrom was blamed for sinking the *France*, the Baron's 1970 challenger, in a gale in the North Sea. When it was learned that Elvstrom had a tendency to suffer mental breakdowns at tense moments, he was dismissed. Bich canceled the Swiss builder, salvaged the *France*, and sent her to Newport with a new skipper, Jean-Marie Le Guillou. It was a good practice effort, but she lost 4-0 to the Australians in the challenger trials.

*Real estate tycoon Alan Bond was 36 when he challenged for the America's Cup.* Lawson's History of the America's Cup.

At 36, Alan Bond, member of the Royal Perth Yacht Club, was the youngest challenger in history. A school dropout, former sign painter and handyman, he was now a real estate developer with business investments in Perth, Western Australia, worth $80 million. Rather than join the privileged class of yacht owners, his attitude was to beat them, and in the process, take them down a few pegs.

It's all very well for the "old money" people in London
and New York to look down their noses at my challenge.
They're the very people who wouldn't hesitate to change the
rules if they thought it might help them. The good old days
when gentlemen could say, "Jolly good show, sir, well done,"
are gone forever. America's Cup racing is far too competitive
for that sort of sentimental nonsense today.

Anyone who considers that racing for the Cup isn't a
business proposition is a bloody fool. There can be no other
justification for spending six million dollars on the Australian challenge unless the return is going to involve more than
just an ornate silver pitcher. Let's see what they say about
commercialism and sportsmanship after we win.

The commercial part of Bond's challenge was aimed at
promoting investment in Yanchep Sun City, his $200 million,
20,000-acre development project thirty-five miles north of Perth.
The development was a barren tract of sand and rocks on which
Bond planned to create a vacation resort with a gigantic marina.
He even brazenly advertised it as the site of the 1977 America's
Cup match. All his expenses for 1974 were written off as advertising costs. To further his interests, Bond commissioned a book
about the 1974 effort and set aside $150,000 for a documentary
film.

More than a year before the match Bond began bolstering
his campaign by making sure his name frequently appeared in
the worldwide press. He informed the NYYC he would protest
even before the races if the defenders were allowed to use a Kev-
lar mainsail (a new, exotic sail cloth). In the autumn of 1973 he
threatened to sue two magazines which published articles describ-
ing his top-secret challenger, the *Southern Cross*. He promised
another protest if any American boat used his boat's innovations.
He alerted the NYYC to the fact that he was bringing his own
lawyer to Newport and a videotape camera crew to record any
infractions.

In the end Alan's threats, allegations and attitude didn't
matter that much. What did matter was the press, especially

*Ben Lexcen was Bond's boat designer.*
Stanley Rosenfeld.

in Australia where home team sympathy was firmly rooted, which gave everyone a chance to read all about it.

Bond's boat was designed by Bob Miller,* whom Bond considered a genius. Lexcen, alias Miller, created the *Southern Cross*, a radical 12-meter with a 70-foot waterline (the longest yet), narrow forward sections, a keel that swept back sharply to a narrow base and a rudder shaped like the bottom part of a tiger shark's tail. She beat the *Gretel* and the *Gretel II* in local trials and easily took the *France* in the challenger trials.

Meanwhile, William J. Strawbridge formed a syndicate for the defense which included veterans of the *Intrepid* years. Sparkman and Stephens was selected as the design team and Bill Ficker was chosen as skipper. Their boat would be the *Courageous*.

In 1973 the Arab-Israeli War and the subsequent oil embargo intervened. Strawbridge asked for a one-year postponement of the Cup match, saying it would be bad for the sport, given the seriousness of the energy crisis. The club denied the request, but not before Bond accused the NYYC of stalling to gain more time. Then the *Courageous* syndicate announced that it was abandoning the project because they only had $600,000. The effects of the oil crisis had dried up their sources. After urging from the NYYC they continued their efforts ten days later. Toward the end of the year the syndicate was reorganized with Robert McCullough as

---

\* Miller changed his name to Ben Lexcen in the early 1970s to escape association with an earlier failed design partnership.

*The* Southern Cross, *center, on her first time out with the* Gretel II *on right, and* Gretel. Lawson's History of the America's Cup.

manager. Ficker had other commitments for the summer and Bob Bavier was made skipper.

Other defending syndicates, with financial problems of their own, began gathering. In the end the *Intrepid* and a radical new boat, the *Mariner*, joined the defender trials. The score was tied 4-4 between the *Courageous* and the *Intrepid* in the final trials when McCullough fired Bavier and made Ted Hood skipper. He won the next race and *Courageous* was selected official defender.

*Ted Hood became skipper of the* Courageous *and guided her through the Cup Races.* Stanley Rosenfeld.

Bond went immediately to the press claiming that the Aussies were apprehensive and concerned:

> We are fearful that fouling and striking tactics will be introduced to America's Cup starts. We deplore this approach which is degrading to the dignity and prestige of the America's Cup as one of the world's most important sporting events and we are most concerned that this style of racing could be condoned by the NYYC ... Apart from the unsportsmanlike nature of this approach there is a definite element of danger to the safety of the crews and boats by adoption of rodeo tactics afloat.

An odd statement from one who earlier proclaimed the value of commercialism over sportsmanship.

The Cup races were again anticlimactic with the defender sweeping in four straight. The times were four minutes, fifty-four seconds; one minute, eleven seconds; five minutes, twenty-seven seconds and seven minutes, nineteen seconds.

Later someone asked "Gentleman Jim" Brady how he slept after the first race.

"Like a baby. Woke up every two hours and cried."

There was a near collision before the second race with both boats raising protest flags. Following the race the newly formed international protest committee disallowed both, although many thought the *Southern Cross* had committed a foul.

Bond said he would be back and returned to Australia to prepare for 1977.

The *Southern Cross* was later converted to a charter yacht by the construction of a toilet and shower, beds, kitchen/galley and dining area. The deck was modified to include two cockpits and a motor was fitted. She provides chartered overnight sailing trips in the Whitsunday Islands, Queensland, Australia.

*The* Courageous *returns home through the salutes of several spectator boats after winning the fourth race.* Stanley Rosenfeld.

*Following the win the entire crew, and even innocent bystanders, were thrown overboard.* Stanley Rosenfeld.

# 24

# SEA CHANGE

B y the 1970s the America's Cup had become big business. The small, clubby syndicate groups created within
the challenging and defending clubs were a thing of the
past. As costs grew beyond the grasp of individual yachtsmen
and yacht clubs, finances fell into the hands of businessmen and
corporations with no connection and little interest in the sport
for its own sake. At the same time the increasing intensity and
complexity of modern campaigns caused challenge and defense
syndicates to become small corporations, independent of their
sponsoring clubs.

Alan Bond foretold the future when he said the traditions
of the America's Cup were "sentimental nonsense" and mounted
an aggressive, businesslike campaign. Soon the challenging and
defending corporate syndicates turned to other businesses outside
the boating industry, and eventually, the general public for funds.

A major milestone during this era came about as the result of a nonstarter in the 1974 Cup match, the California International Sailing Foundation. Before abandoning its plans to enter the defender trials it received a ruling from the Internal Revenue Service that gave it tax-exempt status. In other words, contributors to a defending syndicate could deduct donations from their income taxes. This gave syndicates something tangible to offer potential backers.

In 1977 the corporate sponsors arrived. The Royal Göteburg Yacht Club syndicate let it be known at home that the Cup challenge would be an excellent opportunity to show off Sweden's culture, industry and yachting skill. Volvo led a $2 million campaign, followed by sixty-four other Swedish corporations. They rented three Newport mansions, operated a three-day Export Exhibition and staged concerts with Swedish musicians both there and throughout the rest of the United States, each with a different corporate sponsor. Carl Gustaf, the king of Sweden, became patron of the first national challenge in America's Cup history. Soon Newport was flooded with T-shirts, coffee mugs, postcards, ashtrays and other mementos, each bearing the America's Cup decal.

The reaction of the NYYC was bewilderment. In the spring of 1977 it came to Newport to offer an "approved" array of souvenirs. Then it registered the trademark of the Cup, but didn't protect it. While local merchants were selling ashtrays, coffee mugs, T-shirts, etc., and Swedish industrialists were taking orders for new Volvos and promoting Swedish heritage throughout the country, the NYYC tried to sell cheap curios to Newport shopkeepers. It simply didn't know how to operate in the public arena.

Enter Robert E. (Ted) Turner III, a one man maelstrom in the America's Cup pageantry. Crude, loud, vulgar, outrageous, a braggart, a public drunk and public womanizer, he was also straightforward, unaffected, unpredictable, enthusiastic and frank about his own shortcomings. He was everything the NYYC was not.

After being expelled from Brown University in 1960, he took over his father's Atlanta-based billboard and advertising business at the age of twenty-four. Soon he acquired a cable TV network and the Atlanta professional baseball and basketball teams. For him, learning and entering new ventures meant, "You have to go where the hot stuff is and get whipped."

*Ted Turner, presumably at a news conference, answering questions with panache. His unorthodox style made him a favorite of the media.* Darling.

He followed the same motto when it came to sailing. After two failed efforts with a chartered boat, the *Scylla*, in the Southern Ocean Racing Circuit and the Montego Bay race in the early 1960s, he came back to the SORC a second time in a newly purchased boat, the *Vamp X*, and won by the biggest margin ever. He was hooked. Following several more victories and a few loses, in 1969 he bought the *American Eagle*, the unsuccessful 1964 contender, and sailed her as a trial horse (under a Confederate Flag) against the *Gretel II* in the 1970 challenger trials. By 1974 Ted Turner was thirty-five years old and had sailed more miles in a 12-meter boat than anyone alive. He was the logical choice to skipper a new boat, the *Mariner*, in the defender trials that year. He was denied membership in the NYYC twice before, after alienating some of the club members with his shoreside indiscretions. But, thanks to the urging of the new boat's designer, George Hinman, he was accepted in December 1973. Turner was then named skipper of the *Mariner*. After several trial races (*Valiant* vs. *Mariner*) he was replaced by Dennis Conner. Hinman later said, "His contribution was substantial. But he is an extrovert, he is temperamental, and he wasn't working out on the boat."

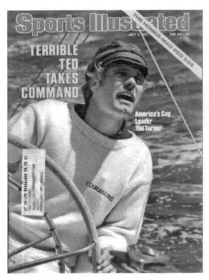

*Upon winning the defender position, Turner was featured on the cover of* Sports Illustrated. www. aidstonavigation.blogspot.com

Disappointed, yet determined, Ted Turner came back in 1977.

After the 1974 Cup match, Turner tried to buy the *Courageous*, but the Kings Point Fund* Syndicate gave it to skipper/sailmaker Ted Hood. Hood asked Alfred Lee Loomis to manage his syndicate which would build a new boat, using the *Courageous* as a trial horse to tune up for the defender trials. For a skipper they needed someone with skill and enough money to make a significant donation. Turner was asked if he was interested. He said he was, but not on those terms, i.e. he and the *Courageous* would be put out to pasture once the new boat entered the defender trials. Turner countered with an offer of his own. He would contribute all the *Courageous'* basic campaign expenses. The syndicate would enter her in the trials as a partner to the new boat, not a trial horse, and Turner would be skipper. Loomis agreed, providing Turner used Hood sails. Turner said no deal, pointing out, "It would be nice to have one amateur out there who wasn't part of the factory team, who was doing it like it had always been done." Loomis reluctantly agreed.

The defender trials were held with three contenders: the *Enterprise*, newly commissioned on the West Coast from Olin Stephens with Lowell North as skipper, using North sails; the newly built *Independence*, skippered by Ted Hood, using Hood

---

*    Affiliated with the U.S. Merchant Marine Academy at Kings Point, New York.

sails; and the *Courageous*, skippered by Ted Turner, sailing by instinct. By the end of June, Turner was ahead with the best win-loss ratio, 7-1. North won five and lost three, while Hood was all but gone with a 0-8 record. Turner hit a slump in July and the others gained slightly. However, by August, Turner had a second wind and his opponents' crews were showing the strain of competition. Despite crew changes on the *Enterprise* and the *Independence*, Turner (with no crew changes) prevailed. Hood was told he was out of the running on August 29, the *Enterprise* received the same message the following day.

A much changed Alan Bond was back for the 1977 match. Subdued, thoughtful, even sportsmanlike, Bond said, "We just brought one boat this time, and all we want to do is win some races. Last time we came here to promote Yanchep. We achieved that purpose (it was sold to the Japanese) and now we're here to

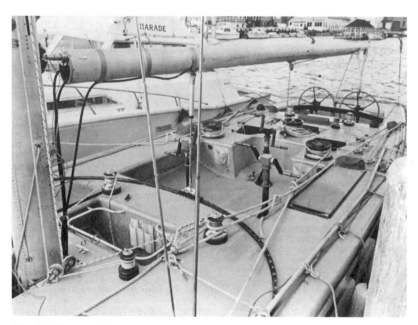

*The deck layout of the* Australia *gives some idea of the complexity of America's Cup boats.* Darling.

*Sweden's entry, the* Sverige *made a good showing in the challenger trials, but lost out to the* Australia. Stanley Rosenfeld.

sail ... I'll enjoy it much more this time. There was too much tension before. And we didn't think we could lose.

"There is a great fascination about competing for and winning such an old sporting event that has never been won by anyone but the Americans. It's like climbing a great mountain."

Bond, operating with a reduced budget of some $1.5 million ($9 million in the previous attempt) and representing the Sun City Yacht Club, had a new boat, the *Australia*. Other challengers included the *Gretel II* for the Royal Sydney Yacht Squadron,

Baron Bich's *France I*, representing the Yacht Club d'Hyeres and the previously mentioned *Sverige*, flying the flag of the Royal Göteborg Yacht Club.

In a best of seven series, the *Australia* easily beat the *France I*. The *Sverige* and the *Gretel II* had a close match, with the Swedish boat winning 4-3. But then *Australia* beat her badly, 4-0.

The America's Cup match pitted the *Australia* against the *Courageous*. The NYYC anticipated twice as many spectator boats for the first race as watched the entire 1974 series. National television networks showed an interest for the first time.

As before, it was a clean sweep, with Turner winning, 4-0. His times were: one minute, forty-eight seconds; one minute, three seconds; two minutes, thirty-two seconds and two minutes, twenty-five seconds.

What set the series apart from all others was the way Ted Turner celebrated it. He had a few beers in him, even before the boat docked after the fourth race. As *Courageous* approached, Turner stood on the bow, a cigar tilted jauntily upward. He bowed,

*A celebrating, and not very sober,* Courageous *crew is about to throw everyone in the water.* The Providence Journal.

left and right, doffing his trademark denim engineer's cap. Once alongside he began drinking champagne, rum, aquavit or all three, depending on who is telling the story. Then his crew threw him into the water.

When later asked how he won, Turner replied, "One, I had the most experience sailing big boats. Two, I was the best organizer and leader. Three, I didn't make a lot of changes. I just concentrated on sailing."

Even then he was already planning for 1980, but fate would have something to say about that.

# 25

# A STUDY IN SKIPPERS

When Ted Turner returned to Newport in 1980, public expectation was for another win. He had the championship boat, the same crew; another round of headlines, jokes, adoring crowds, tough, close races, champagne corks and sopping wet winners was in the offing. But, two factors changed that. First, Turner was the type of man who needed new challenges. He had already won the America's Cup. The gut-burning need to win was satisfied. Now it was just another yacht race — "been there, done that" was the popular phrase.

The second factor was Dennis Conner.

As the son of a commercial fisherman, Conner's childhood was spent within half a block of the San Diego Yacht Club. Although he was an outsider, it fascinated him. He later wrote that experience developed two things in him: an inferiority complex, and the need to overcome same by winning sailboat races.

*Dennis Conner, skipper of the* Freedom, *was known for his exhaustive preparation and methodical approach.* Stanley Rosenfeld.

By the beginning of the 1980 campaign for the Cup, Conner had an enviable record. It included an Olympic bronze medal, two Congressional Cups, two Star Class world championships and two Class A victories in the Southern Ocean Racing Circuit.

In addition he was a journeyman helmsman in the 1974 America's Cup effort in the earlier races of the *Mariner* and the *Courageous*.

He was completely different from Turner. Where Turner was hot and emotional, Conner was cool and organized. While Turner relished being a public figure, Conner cherished his privacy. Make a mistake aboard Turner's boat during a race and you suffered his sudden, loud, brutal wrath, which he quickly forgot. Do the same on Conner's boat and you could not tell he was aware of it. Turner needed assurance. Conner wanted suggestions. Turner needed public adulation. Conner only needed to know he was the best. Turner was the last true sportsman in America's Cup competition. Conner was methodical and determined.

During Conner's early years, crewing other people's boats, he learned about sailing and sailors. Deciding early on that he didn't have a natural talent for sailing, he vowed to overcome it with hard work, long hours, and careful, meticulous preparation. He also found organizing and leading a crew on someone else's boat gave him as much satisfaction as steering in a race. "I would not organize a crew simply by inviting my friends, as Ted did," he revealed. "I would select the best man for each job whether or not I knew him."

By 1980 Conner had a reputation as a very tough, very aggressive helmsman who would do anything within the rules to win. Earlier, just after the 1977 match, he was asked by The Maritime College at Fort Schuyler Foundation to skipper its newly acquired *Enterprise* as a trial horse against either the *Intrepid* or the *Independence* in the next match. He agreed to skipper for them, but on his terms: they would build a new boat, give him a free hand in picking a crew, assure him he would not be fired, and he would sail the new boat against the *Enterprise* <u>and</u> decide which boat he would choose. The syndicate agreed.

Launched in May 1979, the *Freedom* was put to work a month later, nearly a year before his competition began tuning their boats. To develop baseline data, he restored the *Enterprise* to her 1977 form, put her in top condition, and brought back all the 1977 crew to sail her against *Freedom* for ten days.

For his crews, Conner chose twenty-one men from a pool of 120 applicants. Unpaid, nine of them nonetheless had a vested interest in the doings, being sailmakers, suppliers and other such seasoned boating professionals.

Then he began working on the boats in earnest. He moved them from Newport to California so they could work all winter. Conner explained, "We tried to change one thing at a time so we'd know if it was a better solution. And sometimes we changed things back to avoid confusion." He then hired a physical trainer to put his crew through daily exercises before they went out to test each of their more than eighty sails. It was a long, painstakingly slow process, and very professional.

In mid-1980 the challengers arrived at Newport. There was the Swedish entry from 1977, the *Sverige*, with Pelle Petterson at the helm. From Great Britain came Tony Boyden with a new syndicate and the *Lionheart*. Baron Bich, too, returned for the last time with a new boat, the *France III*. The fourth challenger was Alan Bond with an improved *Australia*.

*In the second race* Australia, *foreground, with her bendy rig and expert sailing won. Note the curve in the upper mast.* Stanley Rosenfeld.

The Swedish boat and the British boat were eliminated on August 25, leaving the Australians and the French to decide who would be the challenger. The French put up their best defense in a decade, but, in the end, lost four out of five races to the Aussies.

In the defender's camp, Conner and his two boats had put in an excess of 300 days of sailing — more than twice as much as any challenger or defender. He finally chose the *Freedom* for the defender trials and won forty-two of forty-seven races. She would be the defender for the Cup. A distracted Ted Turner (he was spending more than $2 million a month building up his TV station) and *Courageous* were eliminated on August 25. The *Clipper*, skippered by 24-year-old Russel Long and a crew of newcomers, was eliminated on August 29.

As the *Australia* and the *Freedom* approached the starting line for the first race, Conner had one nagging concern. It was the "bendy" mast on the Australian boat. Brought over with the British *Lionheart*, it was quickly copied and installed on the *Australia*. The upper part of the mast had a flexible tip that could be bent back when sailing to windward to increase the sail area by some

*First day of issue envelope commemorating* Freedom's *win over* Australia.
www.thesaltysailor.com

100 square feet without exceeding the limits of the measurement rules. Those who saw it in operation said it produced a significant increase in a boat's speed.

Despite the "bendy" mast, Conner simply got better starts and he and his crew sailed flawlessly. Conner and the *Freedom*, took the Cup. The *Australia* won the second race by twenty-eight seconds, but lost four others.

*The challenging yacht as she appears today.* Frank Lagudi.

# 26

# THE YEAR AMERICA
# LOST THE CUP

Ten challenges were submitted to the NYYC after the
1980 Cup match, more than for any match in the entire
132-year history of the event. Of these, seven competed:
three from Australia and one each from Great Britain, France,
Canada and Italy. The overwhelming turnout was because Australia came so close during the 1980 races. They won one race,
almost won another, and stayed in contention until the very end.
This despite presenting an underfunded challenge against the
strongest defense ever presented. The year 1983 was, as Samuel
Johnson said of second marriages, a triumph of optimism over
experience.

   Part of the reason there were so many challengers was that
by 1983, yacht design outside the United States had caught up
to that within. In addition, the rules again changed (including
making the "bendy mast" disallowed after the 1980 match) and

the Deed of Gift was re-interpreted. Challengers were no longer restricted to equipment and facilities from their own country. They could shop for materials anywhere, including the United States, where state-of-the-art Mylar/Kevlar sails were available. The net result was very little difference between the boats of challengers and defenders. The match of 1983 would be determined by skill, training and, possibly, a bit of luck.

Would that it were that straightforward.

An additional factor was that the America's Cup had become an irresistible publicity event. Thanks to Sir Frank Packer, Alan Bond and Ted Turner, journalists were drawn to the Cup races by the participant's forceful personalities. Where the press corps numbered 192 for the 1937 match, in 1983 there were almost 1,400. Every boat syndicate had backing from national and international corporations wanting the benefits of being part of a high-profile event. Their ever expanding interest was fed by dollars and media exposure.

The challengers were a fascinating group. From Italy the Costa Smeralda Yacht Club, backed by eighteen blue-chip corporations and led by the Aga Khan, brought the *Azzura I* and surprised everyone with their racing acumen.

The French syndicate was a different matter. Headed by soft-porn producer Yves Rousset-Rouard, it fielded Baron Bich's well-used *France III,* but not Bich, nor a trial horse, nor money, nor any real hope of winning.

Cutting a broad swath were the British with the *Victory 83.* Their syndicate was under the guidance of a thirty-eight-year-old prep school dropout, multi-millionaire businessman named Peter de Savary, who had a liking for expensive champagne, large Havana cigars, headlines, fast cars, fast boats, his own opinions and winning. Although at least one other syndicate had a faster boat, nobody left a broader wake.

From Canada came the *Canada I,* launched by lawyer Marvin McDill and a group of businessmen from Calgary. After the

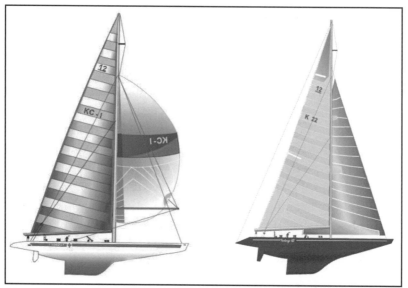

*Line drawings of two of the contenders,* Canada 1, *left, and* Victory 83, *give an example of the hull form and rigs of some of the challengers.* K. Urtz.

NYYC accepted its challenge, the team lost its yacht club sponsor and had to establish its own club, The Secret Cove Yacht Club. The Canadian syndicate then became the Secret Cove Yacht Club Challenge. Their misfortune continued when the boat-builder decided he would not release the yacht before its bill was paid. But this difficulty was eventually overcome. Nonetheless, the syndicate continued to run out of money and had several mechanical problems with their contender.

One of the three Australian syndicates also had problems. The *Advance*, of the Royal Sydney Yacht Squadron was notoriously slow, which generated a bit of humor, but only two wins. More than one writer nicknamed her the Down Underdog. Someone else scheduled an appointment for her with a local veterinarian. In July, after her first victory in twenty attempts, her crew painted the face of a dog on her bow, with the intent of adding an additional feature after each subsequent win. They never got past the whiskers.

Alan Bond, returning yet again, challenged through the Royal Perth Yacht Club. He originally planned a two-boat offense: the *Challenge 12* and the *Australia II*. When this became too problematic, he sold the plans for the first boat to Richard Pratt, a wealthy box manufacturer. Pratt then challenged under the flag of the Royal Yacht Club of Victoria.

More has been written about the winged keel of the *Australia II* than anything in America's Cup history. It was original, kept secret and very effective. The concept was relatively simple; under the 12-Meter rule it is advantageous to lower the center of gravity of the boat by keeping the weight of the keel as low as possible. A simple bulb attached to the bottom of the keel to lower the weight would cause extra resistance through the water. A wing shape can improve performance, if correctly designed, without increasing resistance. Designer Ben Lexcen developed such a winged keel, tested it at the Ship Model Basin in Wageningen, The Netherlands, and added it to the *Australia II*. By the time the other syndicates heard of the new keel, in June 1983, it was too late for them to design and fit such a device on their own boats. Some attempts were made to attach small wings, or winglets, to existing boats' keels without success.

The Australian boat was measured early in the season along with the other competing boats by the official measurers: an American, an Australian, and an Englishman. The three measurers agreed that the Australian boat, as well as all the others in the competition, were proper 12-Meter boats. They had no further comment. The NYYC then tried to show that wings were unacceptable under the 12-Meter rule. Their attempt failed. They followed this with an attempt to show that the keel was designed by non-Australians in The Netherlands, another violation of the rules. This also failed. In the end they had to fight it out, one race at a time, on the water.

The challengers went through a series of trials off Newport that were dominated by *Australia II* skippered by John Bertrand, Olympic and Australian championship veteran. For the first time luxury luggage-producer Louis Vuitton donated a Cup and sponsored and named these elimination races the Louis Vuitton Cup. With the first round of races the *Challenge 12,* the *Advance* and the *France III* were eliminated. In the semi-finals the *Canada I* and the *Azzura I* were left behind. The final was between *Australia II* and *Victory 83*, with, of course, Alan Boyd's boat the victor.

The defenders put six boats through selection trials, four of them new. The Freedom 83 syndicate, with Dennis Conner as skipper, commissioned the *Spirit of America* from Sparkman and Stephens, and the *Magic* from Johan Valentijn. Gary Johnson and Tom Blackaller commissioned a new *Defender* from Dave Pedrick and rebuilt the old *Courageous*. In a trial held in 1982 none of the new boats were a match for the *Courageous* and the *Freedom* from 1980. Conner then commissioned the *Liberty* from Valentijn and she became the defender.

*This photo shows the* Australia II *out of the water and the winged keel to good advantage.* Dan Nerney.

The Cup match took place between September 13 and 26. A best of seven series, it was the first time all seven races were necessary.

The first race, on September 14, gave each skipper a chance to gauge his opponent. The *Australia II* won the start, and surprised Conner with its performance in the first two legs. The Aussies then had steering problems and the *Liberty* took the next

*John Bertrand will always be remembered as the first challenger to win the America's Cup. He was known for his relaxed confidence.* Robert P. Foley.

four legs and the race by one minute, ten seconds.

Australia tore a sail in the second race, but had the lead in the second, third and fourth legs, only to lose to the United States by one minute, thirty-three seconds.

The third race extended beyond the time limit and was rerun on September 18. The *Australia II* dominated and shocked the Americans, winning six of seven legs and the race by an astonishing three minutes, fourteen seconds.

In the third race the *Liberty*, Conner, and her crew proved their mettle, winning all seven legs and the race by forty-three seconds. The score was now 3-1, with only one more win needed to retain the Cup. The American team felt confident. During an interview, Conner remarked, "God must be an American."

But Australia came back in the fifth race to win by one minute, forty-seven seconds.

The sixth race was again a walkover for the Australians, winning by a resounding three minutes, twenty-five seconds. The score was now tied at 3.

The seventh race was marked by milestones: since the beginning of the 12-Meter era, challengers had won only three of thirty-five America's Cup races, the *Australia II* won three in one match. Conner became the first skipper in the 132-year history of the Cup to sail all seven races. Although the Americans lead from the start to the fourth mark, the Aussies soon gained the lead and won by forty-one seconds. For the first time ever, the America's Cup belonged to another country.

In the aftermath of the win much was made of the Australians secret winged keel and the psychological effect the knowledge of its existence had on the American team. But a lot of the credit belongs to John Bertrand, the Australian skipper, and his team both ashore and afloat. Dennis Conner commented that the brilliant supporting organization behind Bertrand

This cartoon appeared in an Australian newspaper after the first race. The blazers and straw hats are the "uniform" of NYYC officials. The Herald, Melbourne, Australia.

probably did more to "faze" the Americans than any other single factor.

Conner was not finished. He would return.

Alan Bond was overjoyed to accept the America's Cup from the New York Yacht Club at ceremonies in the Newport mansion formerly owned by Harold Vanderbilt. Providence Journal.

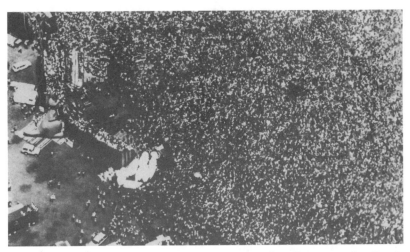

*A gigantic crowd greeted the* Australia II*'s crew when they arrived in Perth.*
AP.

*According to this cartoon, with the America's Cup in the hands of the*
*Australians, its place was taken in the trophy case by Dennis Conner's head.*
The Northern Territory News, Darwin, Australia.

# 27

# PASSING THE CUP

At about 8 P.M. on September 27, 1983, the America's Cup, considered by many the Holy Grail of yachting, was unbolted from its display case, placed in a black box, carried out the front door of the NYYC, and placed in a waiting Brinks truck. A small group of onlookers, despite the solemn, tear-stained faces of club officials, happily sang a chorus of "Waltzing Matilda."

By the following day, the newly-polished Cup gleamed in the sunlight on the veranda of Marble House, Harold Vanderbilt's former home in Newport. Commodore Stone, of the NYYC, first handed Alan Bond the forty-inch bolt that had fastened the Cup to its table. "We don't want Alan to keep this for 132 years, but we thought he ought to have it," Stone said.

Then he remarked that Ben Lexcen once said that if the Aussies won the Cup they would hire a steamroller, squash it flat, and create the Australian plate. "No need to do that," said Stone, the NYYC had done it for them. He held up a battered Plymouth hubcap, suggesting it had great historical significance in the United States as it commemorated the landing of the Pilgrims. He handed the hubcap to Lexcen.

Commodore Stone then turned the Cup itself over to Peter Dalziell, commodore of the Royal Perth Yacht Club who said, "The Cup will have pride of place in our clubhouse, and I welcome any challengers to the summer of 1987." Stone assured him that the NYYC would be there.

Quite suddenly, the Royal Perth Yacht Club found itself in the position of defender of the Cup, with all that entailed. It now had to arrange accommodations for boats and crews from around the world, run the races, mount a defense, be hospitable, and, most importantly, deal with squabbling challengers and defenders on the subject of television rights.

The Cup was put on display in an art gallery in Perth where, within a few weeks, it was seen by more people than had viewed it during its entire 132-year history in New York. The Western Australia Tourism Commission hired skipper John Bertrand as "roving ambassador" to help promote the coming event, valued at a billion dollars in revenue. A Western Australian tourism minister announced that federal and state governments would finance the construction in Perth of a large convention center, including "the biggest and best gambling casino in the world."

By early 1986, seven major hotels, two marinas and hundreds of other tourist related projects were being built in the Perth/Fremantle area. Alan Bond was planning a luxury hotel in Perth

*Vehicle license plates announced Western Australia as the "Home of the America's Cup."* en.wikipedia.org

and a forty-five-unit townhouse development in Fremantle. He ordered a new $10 million flagship with a heli-pad on the top deck for the Bond corporation. He also bought another brewery, cornering forty-five percent of the Aussie beer supply. Ten luxury cruise ships signed up to serve as floating hotels and observation platforms for the races.

Then came the next crop of challengers. By the filing deadline of April 1984 the Royal Perth Yacht Club had twenty-four challenges on record. It was almost twenty-five. "We got a call from Saudi Arabia," said a spokesman. "They were interested in challenging, but they didn't have a yacht club. They thought they could buy one of ours." The Saudis were told that was against the rules.

As 1987 approached the field was down to fourteen challengers and four defenders.

From Italy came two challengers. Representing Yacht Club Italiano, the oldest sailing club in Italy (founded in 1897), was the *Italia*. Skippered by Aldo Migliaccio, her syndicate was Consorzio Italia. After placing third in the semi-finals in 1983, the *Azzura* was back. Again she represented the Costa Smeralda Yacht Club. Her syndicate was Azzura and her skipper Lorenzo Bortolotti.

France entered two challengers. From the Societe des Regates Rochelaises came the *French Kiss*, built by the syndicate Challenge KIS France and skippered by Marc Pujot. She was

*The* French Kiss *was computer designed and performed surprisingly well.* www.martin-raget.com

the first 12-meter boat designed entirely by computer and built without being tank-tested. This gave her the advantage of not having her technical specifications available to other syndicates. In addition she was considered highly sophisticated. Representing the Societe Nautique de Marseille were the *France 3* and the *Challenge 12*. Both boats belonged to the syndicate Challenge Francais pour L'America's Cup which was backed by the mayor of Marseilles.

The Secret Cove Yacht Club returned again with the *Canada II*, built by the Canada II Syndicate. At the same time the Royal Nova Scotia Yacht Squadron offered the *True North* created for the True North Syndicate. Neither syndicate was able to attract sufficient financial backing, so they joined forces for a combined effort. In the end the *Canada II* was the only Canadian boat sent to Fremantle.

From Great Britain came the veteran Royal Thames Yacht Squadron (who made the first challenge for the cup in 1870). Their

*The* Canada II *during the challenger eliminations off Fremantle in 1987. She was sponsored by the Secret Cove Yacht Club, which had been in America's Cup matches before.* www.12mrclass.com

challenge was for The America's Cup Syndicate, contending with the *White Crusader I* and *White Crusader II*.* The *Crusader I* was a traditional design, evolved from the British *Victory '83* of the previous Cup match, while the *Crusader II* was more radical. The second boat was used as a trial horse against the first, but the first was chosen by the team as challenger.

New Zealand entered with the *New Zealand (KZ 7)*, unique amongst all other contenders because of her fiberglass hull (the others were aluminum). Nicknamed the "Kiwi Magic," she was highly competitive and made a respected name for herself. She represented either the Royal New Zealand Yacht Squadron or the Mercury Bay Boating Club (sources vary), her syndicate was New Zealand's America's Cup Challenge and her skipper was Chris Dickson.

The United States offered six challengers. From Chicago came the *Heart of America* and the *Clipper,* under the auspices of the Chicago Yacht Club. Their syndicate was Heart of America Challenge, Inc. and their leading skipper was Harry C. "Buddy" Melges, Jr. The Newport Harbor Yacht Club Los Angeles sent the *Eagle*, built by The Eagle Syndicate and skippered by Rod Davis. A very determined New York Yacht Club challenged with *America II*, funded by the America II Challenge syndicate, with John Kolius as skipper. From the San Diego Yacht Club came *Liberty*, *Stars & Stripes 83*, *Stars and Stripes 85*, *Stars and Stripes 86* and *Stars and Stripes 87*. Their syndicate, with a $12 million fund (later estimates show $16 million), was the Sail America Foundation and their leading skipper an obsessed-with-winning Dennis Conner. Northern California entered with the *USA II*, built by the St. Francis Challenge America's Cup 1987 with a $10 million budget, and skippered by Tom Blackaller. Finally, the Yale Corinthian Yacht Club brought back the veteran *Courageous IV*

---

\*    Originally named *Crusader I* and *Crusader II*, the prefix "White" was added after millionaire Graham Walker, owner of White Horse whiskey, contributed heavily to the syndicate at the last minute.

*The KZ 7,* Kiwi Magic, *her keel shrouded in secrecy, is lowered into the water.* www.expeterra.com

(now fitted with a winged keel). Her syndicate was The Courageous Syndicate and her skippers, David Vietor and Peter Isler.

Four groups defended the America's Cup for Australia. Alan Bond was back for the fifth time and now with the home field advantage. His two boats, the *Australia III* and the *Australia IV* (with an improved winged keel), sailed for the Royal Perth Yacht Club. Their syndicate was America's Cup Defence 1987 Ltd. and their leading skipper Colin Beasbel. Sailing for the same club were the *Kookaburra,* the *Kookaburra II* and the *Kookaburra III.* The latter boat was described as a "fully-blown, radical 12-meter" hi-tech yacht. Their syndicate was Taskforce 1987 Defence and their skipper Iain Murray. From the Royal South Australian Yacht Squadron came the *South Australia,* built by the South Australian Challenge for the Defence of the America's Cup 1987 syndicate, with Phil Thompson as their skipper. The Royal Sydney Yacht Squadron presented the *Steak 'N Kidney* as their defender, her syndicate was the Eastern Australia Defence Syndicate for the America's Cup. Their boat made a surprisingly good showing, reaching the semi-finals in the defender eliminations.

The money backing the 1987 America's Cup match had grown exponentially. Where in 1983 corporate funding accounted for five percent of the syndicates' funding, this time corporations covered fifty percent. In 1983 all the participants spent less than

$18 million. The projection for 1987 was $150 million. Part of this increased expense was simply that there were twice as many challengers, three times as many boats and four times as many designers.

First came the elimination races to determine which boat would be the final challenger and which the final defender.

For the challengers, this meant the Louis Vuitton Cup. First a series of round robin* tournaments were held to determine the finalists. These were structured so that each boat raced against every other boat in a series of three races. In the first round robin three boats finished with 11-1 records: the *America II* of the New York Yacht Club, the *Stars and Stripes 87* and the KZ 7 (*Kiwi Magic*). The second round saw Conner's *Stars and Stripes 87* struggle. She lost to Tom Blackaller and the *USA II* in light winds, and the following day to the KZ 7. On the ninth day she lost again to the British *White Crusader 1* in light airs, and a day later to the *Canada II*. The Kiwis dominated, winning all eleven of their match races, while the *America II* made a strong showing with a 9-2 record. The third round again belonged to the New Zealand boat which handily defeated the NYYC's *America II*. The New York Yacht Club was eliminated for the first time in Cup history. The *USA II* with her unique design (two rudders, one fore and one aft, and a bulbous bow) showed winning potential and Marc Pajot's *French Kiss* upset the *America II* to make her way into the semi-finals. The KZ 7 was the top qualifier of the round robins, followed in the points competition by *Stars & Stripes 87, USA II* and *French Kiss*.

In the Challenger semi-finals the KZ 7 easily defeated the *French Kiss* 4-0. Meanwhile, a hard fought battle between the *Stars and Stripes 87* and the *USA II* ensued, which Conner won 4-0.

Going into the Louis Vuitton Finals, the *Kiwi Magic* (KZ 7) was the favorite. A fast boat in both light and heavy air, she had

---

\* The term is derived from the word *ruban*, meaning "ribbon." Over a long period of usage, the term evolved to "robin."

beaten the *Stars and Stripes 87* twice, and won thirty-seven of thirty-eight match races. But the American boat was showing her best form of the regatta, particularly in heavy winds above 20 knots.

The first two races were similar, with the *Stars and Stripes 87* going out to an early lead, and holding it on the downwind legs while extending it on the upwind portions. In the third race the American boat rounded the first windward mark 26 seconds ahead. Then she lost her spinnaker. The Kiwis closed the gap and were able to slide ahead on the turn around the mark. Once there they proved a difficult boat to get past and maintained the lead to win the race. The fourth race saw the KZ 7 experience a number of structural failures including losing her backstay and she lost by 3 minutes 38 seconds. In the fifth race the *Stars & Stripes 87* took the initial lead on the first windward leg, but on her second beat to windward her Number 6 genoa blew to pieces and the Kiwis closed the gap. She hoisted another genoa and held on to the slimmest of leads throughout the next four legs. Rounding the final mark she held a six-second lead, which she maintained. The *Stars & Stripes 87* took the series, four wins to one.

Following the completion of the race, Gianfranco Alberini, Commodore, Yacht Club Costa Smeralda, the Challenge Club of

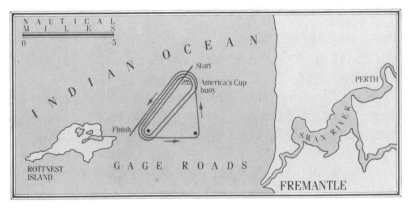

*A modified Olympic course was used for the 1987 series. At twenty-four miles it was the same length as that used since 1964, but with more, and shorter, legs.* Sail Magazine.

*In a surprising upset, the* Kookaburra III *defeated the* Australia IV *to become the defender. For the first time in thirteen years, Alan Bond would not be in the final Cup match.* www.12mrclass.com

Record responsible for organizing the challenger selection process had at last completed his responsibilities.

"We have concluded today two hundred and twenty-three races. ... very successful for sure, selecting the two best yachts for the finals of the Louis Vuitton Cup, and the best challenger for the America's Cup 87."

The series to determine the defender was far less dramatic. After a series of round robin races, a Defender Finals contest was sailed between Alan Bond's *Australia IV* and the *Kookaburra III*, with the *Kookaburra III* sweeping the finals in five races to become the defender. For the first time in thirteen years Alan Bond was eliminated from the competition for the America's Cup.

As was often the case over the years when the NYYC hosted the cup, the America's Cup match itself was a bit "ho-hum." Dennis Conner and the *Stars & Stripes 87* took four straight races in the best of seven series with times of: one minute, forty-one seconds; one minute, ten seconds; one minute, forty-six seconds and one minute, fifty-nine seconds.

The next host for the America's Cup would be San Diego, California.

*To build the fastest boat possible, three designers were taken on to develop the* Stars and Stripes *'87. Nothing was left to chance in the quest for the Cup.* Sail Magazine.

*A tired, but very happy, Dennis Conner with the America's Cup in 1987.* Sail Magazine.

*A cartoon image summarizies the outcome.* www.ebay.com

# 28

# DAVID VS. GOLIATH

Michael Fay, a wealthy banker, had backed New Zealand's first America's Cup campaign in 1987. In 1988, as head of a new America's Cup challenge syndicate, representing the Mercury Bay Boating Club, he lodged a challenge to the San Diego Yacht Club that caught the Americans by surprise. Rather than wait three to four years, he had his legal team review the original Deed of Gift for the America's Cup. The deed did not specify a time delay between challenges, nor were competitors limited to compete in a particular class of boat, nor did boats have to be the same size or class. Fay financed the creation of *New Zealand* (KZ 1), a large single-hull yacht which complied with the Deed of Gift but was much larger, at the maximum allowed ninety feet on the waterline, and faster, than the 12-meter boats which were used for so many years.

The San Diego Yacht Club dismissed the challenge out of hand. Fay then took the issue to the New York State Supreme Court,

*The* New Zealand *was unusually large. Note the main deck "wings" to give the crew extra leverage in balancing the boat.* www. homepage2. nifty.com

which on November 25, 1987, declared it valid and instructed the San Diego Yacht Club to meet the challenge on the water, brushing aside the twenty-one 12-meter syndicates that declared their intention of racing in a 1991 America's Cup regatta.

Taking a page from Fay's book, the Sail America Foundation, representing the SDYC, decided to also follow the original Deed of Gift. As all the rules pertained to waterline length, and none addressed the number of hulls used in a boat, they built a catamaran, the *Stars and Stripes.*

On May 5, 1988 Michael Fay returned to court, seeking a ruling that the catamaran was an invalid defender because the two boats were totally unalike. The court instead ruled that, as there was nothing in the Deed of Gift to prevent the race from happening, the Cup should be contested on the water, and any further legal action should be delayed until after the race.

The New Zealand challenger, *New Zealand* (KZ 1), was a 90-foot monohull with a crew of thirty to forty and skippered by David Barnes. She was launched in March 1988 and

*Samoa issued a special coin to commemorate the event.* www. colnect.com

regarded as the fastest monohull at that time for her size.

The San Diego Yacht Club, through the Sail America Foundation, responded by building two catamarans for Dennis Conner, one with a conventional soft sail, the *Stars & Stripes* (S 1), and the second with a Scaled Composites-built wing mast, the *Stars & Stripes* (H 3). The wing-masted boat demonstrated superior performance, and after being modified to improve its structural integrity was chosen for the defense.

*Dennis Conner and his two* Stars and Stripes *practicing for the event.* www. chevaliertaglang.blogspot.com

The America's Cup match was to be the best three races held September 7 to 9, 1988 off San Diego, California. The first race was forty nautical miles long, with one windward leg and a return downwind. The second race was a triangular course of thirty-nine nautical miles, with a thirteen mile windward leg, and two thirteen-mile reaching legs. The spectator fleet was the smallest seen in years. The *Stars & Stripes* won the first race by eighteen minutes and fifteen seconds and the second by twenty-one minutes and ten seconds. It was the shortest America's Cup competition since 1887.

Following the races the battle returned to the courts. On March 28, 1989 the cup was awarded to New Zealand. The court's reasoning was the competition between a monohull and a catamaran was a gross mismatch and not in the spirit of friendly competition between countries. However the Appellate Division reversed that ruling, saying the Deed of Gift does not limit design nor say anything about the number of hulls a yacht may have.

*The size difference is apparent as the two contenders run side by side. Note the crew of the* New Zealand *leaning outboard on the starboard side.* Rosenfeld Collection Mystic Seaport Museum.

The reversal was confirmed on April 26, 1990 by the New York Court of Appeals.

San Diego retained the cup and would defend it again in 1992.

# 29

# THE CLASS OF '92

To eliminate the contention, lawsuits, and "apples and oranges" differences in competing yachts in the 1988 Cup series, a new class of boat was developed for the America's Cup in 1992. Termed the International America's Cup Class (IACC), its purpose was to produce boats similar to one another built to the same formula, yet allowing designers the freedom to experiment.

The formula was:

$$\frac{L + 1.25 \times \sqrt{S} - 9.8 \times \sqrt[3]{DSP}}{0.686} \leq 24.000\,\text{meters}$$

DSP: displacement in cubic meters
L: rated length in meters
S: rated sail area in square meters

In general, America's Cup boats would have the following specifications: length, 82 feet (25 meters); weight: 24 tonnes (24 long tons; 26 short tons); height of the mast: 115 feet (35 meters); sail surface area: 389 sq. yd. (325 square meters) upwind, 900 sq. yd. (750 square meters) downwind.

Designs for the new class began well before the 1992 competition. As early as 1988 Il Moro di Venezia laid down plans for the first of five boats built for the 1992 Italian team, Il Moro Challenge. Headed by billionaire industrialist Raul Gardini, the Italian team was truly international in character and typical of the direction toward which America's Cup racing was moving. The principal designer was Argentine naval architect German Frers, assisted by American Robert Hopkins. The yard director was Portuguese, Fernando Sena, the operations manager was French, Laurent Esquier and the skipper was French-American Paul Cayard.

The first boat built under the new IACC specifications, the *Il Moro di Venezia I* (ITA 1), was launched on March 11, 1990 in Venice. She was followed by the *Il Moro di Venezia II* (ITA 7), launched on August 7, 1990 in Palma de Mallora. Then came the *Il Moro di Venezia III* (ITA 15), launched on April 15, 1991 in San Diego, the *Il Moro di Venezia IV* (ITA 16), launched on June 15, 1991 in San Diego and finally, the *Il Moro di Venezia V* (ITA 25), launched on December 16, 1991 in San Diego.

The cost of the Italian effort was estimated at $85 million. The total amount spent by all eight challengers for the Louis Vuitton Cup was $250 million. In addition to the Italians, the challengers included: the Cruising Yacht Club of Australia sponsoring team Australia Challenge with Syd Fischer as skipper of AUS 17*; the Darling Harbour Yacht Club with their team Spirit of Australia featuring skipper Peter Gilmour as commander of AUS 21; from Spain, the Monte Real Club de Yates de Bayona

---

\* Beginning in 1992 it became increasingly common to refer to boats by their sail number rather than their name and syndicates as "teams."

with team Desafio España Copa America with skipper Pedro Campos Calvo-Sotelo in command of ESP-22; the French challenge came from the Yacht Club de Sète sponsoring team Le Defi Francais 95 with Marc Pajot as skipper of the FRA 27; the first ever Japanese entry from the Nippon Ocean Racing Club offered team Nippon Challenge with New Zealander Chris Dickson as skipper of the JPN 26; returning for New Zealand was the Mercury Bay Boating Club and team New Zealand Challenge with skipper Rod Davis commanding NZL 20; and

*Artist's rendering of the 1992 French challenger* Ville de Paris. *K. Urtz.*

finally from Sweden came the Stenungsbaden Yacht Club featuring team Swedish America's Cup Challenge with skipper Gunnar Krantz at the helm of SWE 19.

Meanwhile, the San Diego Yacht Club began to sort out who would defend the America's Cup. A new form of defending competition was created, mirroring the earlier Louis Vuitton Cup races. In 1992, two defense syndicates (featuring five IACC yachts) competed through four round robins to earn a berth in the Citizen Cup* finals. The winner of the final then became the America's Cup defender of record.

There appeared on the defender's side a formidable force; billionaire Bill Koch. An MIT graduate with bachelor's, master's

---

\* Sponsored by the Citizen Watch Co., Ltd. of Japan.

*The* America³ *during the 1992 Cup match.* www.solarnavigator.net

and doctoral degrees in chemical engineering, he reportedly spent approximately $65 million on four boats in his effort, and though an amateur, sailed as part of the crew himself, assisted by veteran sailors such as Buddy Melges. His syndicate was titled the America³ (pronounced "America cubed") Foundation.

There were five yachts in the Citizen Cup finals, all vying to represent the San Diego Yacht Club. They included: the *Jayhawk* (USA 9) for the America³ Foundation, the *Defiant* (USA 18) representing the America³ Foundation, the *America³* (USA 23) built by the America³ Foundation, *Kanza* (USA 28) also for the America³ Foundation, and the *Stars & Stripes* (USA 11) of Team Dennis Conner.

Three round robin events were run in the Louis Vuitton Cup to decide which teams and boats would be in the semi-finals. In the first round robin, each win was given one point. In the second each win produced four points. Eight points were awarded winners in the third round robin. The top four challengers were Nippon Challenge with 82 points, New Zealand Challenge with

74 points, Il Moro di Venezia
with 69 points and France Le
Defi Francais 95 with sixty-one
points.

The top four then competed
in the semi-finals with New
Zealand Challenge and Il Moro
di Venezia placing first and second. These two squared off in the
final with New Zealand taking
three of the first four races. The
fifth race was nullified when the
Italians protested New Zealand's
bowsprit. Il Moro di Venezia
then took the next four races,
winning the Louis Vuitton Cup

*The Italian Contender* Il Moro di
Venezia II *off San Diego in 1992.*
www.afyacht.com

*The* America³ *leading during the final Cup race.* www.afyacht.com

5-3 and becoming the official challenger for the 1992 America's Cup.

Competition for the Citizen Cup began with a series of four round robin races. This resulted in the *America³*, with two firsts and one second, facing Dennis Conner's *Stars and Stripes*, with one first and three seconds. In the final, a series of eleven races were held. The winner was *America³*, seven to four.

The America's Cup match was held off San Diego in May of 1992. The first race was held on May 9 and won by *America³* crossing the finish line thirty seconds ahead. The Italians came back in the second race, winning by a scant three seconds. The remaining three races were taken by *America³* with times of one minute, fifty-eight seconds; one minute, four seconds; and forty-four seconds in the final race on May 16. The America's Cup remained with the San Diego Yacht Club.

*The* America³ *comes alongside after winning the final race and the America's Cup.* en.wikipedia.org

# 30

# THE SLAUGHTER

# ON THE WATER

B y 1995 it was clear that corporate sponsorship had grown to immense proportions. Of course it was all about developing name recognition on a global scale. And what better way for a company to enhance its image than to advertise itself as the "official" whatever (boatbuilder, designer, sailmaker, roadster, whiskey, beer, wristwatch, T-shirt, etc.) of the America's Cup. But what came to the fore in the 1990s was the realization that there were all those television cameras aimed at the America's Cup yachts, streaming constant video to a worldwide audience. Here was a way to make the company name familiar to the population of the entire globe. All one had to do was plaster one's logo on every hull, sail and crew jacket in the competition. And plaster they did. The 1995 America's Cup competition "showed" more corporate sponsorship than ever before.

Nonetheless it was still a passionate sporting competition featuring the best crews and yachts in the world. Originally ten challengers from seven nations bid to compete for the 1995 Louis Vuitton Cup. Unfortunately, Il Moro di Venezia collapsed and withdrew after its director, Raul Gardini, committed suicide following his involvement in a financial scandal.* The Challenger of Record Committee canceled a Russian bid after it missed several deadlines. The French challenge representing Yacht Club d'Antibes withdrew even though its yacht *Harmony* was almost completed.

This left seven clubs as challengers. The Royal New Zealand Yacht Squadron sponsored Team New Zealand with Russell Coutts as skipper. They brought two boats, the NZL 32 and the NZL 38. The Southern Cross Yacht Club was represented by team One Australia with John Bertrand as skipper. They offered two yachts, the AUS 31 and the AUS 35. Also from Australia was the Cruising Yacht Club of Australia with their team, Sydney 95, featuring Syd Fischer as the skipper of AUS 29. From Spain came the Monte Real Club de Yates de Bayona with team Spanish Challenge and skipper Pedro Campos Calvo-Sotelo on ESP 42. The French were represented by the Yacht Club de Sète and team France America 95 whose skipper, Marc Pajot, had at his disposal the boats FRA 33 and FRA 37. The Japanese returned under the Nippon Yacht Club with team Nippon Challenge whose skipper Makoto Namba sailed the JPN 30 and the JPN 41. The seventh entrant was also from New Zealand under the Tutukaka South Pacific Yacht Club with team Tag Heuer Challenge featuring Chris Dickson as skipper of the NZL 39.

Team New Zealand was headed by Peter Blake. The skipper was Russell Coutts and the crew included Brad Butterworth, Tom Schnackenberg, Murray Jones and Craig Monk. The team was the first challenge from the Royal New Zealand Yacht Squadron but

---

\* However, he left a legacy. In 1995 each team was limited to no more than two IACC boats in competition.

built on the work of three previous challengers. Co-designed by Doug Peterson and Laurie Davidson, their boat showed a significant jump forward in speed. In sea trials against New Zealand's 1992 entry, NZL 20, the new black boat easily outpaced her. Doug Peterson recalled, "That first day Brad Butterworth came back and said, 'My god, it's like a different class of boat.'"

Team One Australia was skippered by John Bertrand, the winner of the 1983 America's Cup. The syndicate won the 1994 IACC World Championship with AUS 31. AUS 35 was then constructed through a partnership agreement with the Australian Challenge.

The Syd Fischer challenge from Sydney, was Fischer's fourth America's Cup entrant.

Spanish Challenge was the last team to arrive in San Diego. Having financial difficulties, they could not build on the 1992 campaign. They had one boat, ESP 42.

From Yacht Club de Sete and skippered by Marc Pajot, France America '95 failed to live up to expectations. *France 2* (FRA 33) was damaged while it was being launched in December 1994 and then the keel fell off in February while she was testing a new sail.

Nippon Challenge built on the 1992 campaign to enter two teams in the 1994 IACC World Championships and have a strong team in the 1995 Cup. The helmsman was John Cutler.

*Nippon Challenge tried, without success, to build on their 1992 experience. Note the abundance of corporate logos. K. Urtz.*

The Tutukaka Challenge was run on a shoestring budget that saw the team nearly not make it to San Diego until the intervention of watchmaker Tag Heuer. Led by Chris Dickson, the crew included Peter Lester, Mike Sanderson and Denis Kendall.

Meanwhile, the American boats gathered for the 1995 Citizen Cup, to determine which boat would defend the trophy for the United States. Three defense syndicates (featuring four IACC yachts) would compete in four round robins, a semi-finals series and the Citizen Cup finals. The winner would defend the America's Cup against the winner of the Louis Vuitton Cup.

In addition to *America³,* Bill Koch chose to defend with the *Mighty Mary*, crewed entirely by women. When first announced in March 1994 the team attracted over 600 applicants. Of these, 120 were tested on board. Finally a crew of thirty was selected. It included sport sailors, rowers and weight lifters, the latter because the handling of the "coffeegrinder" winches for the sails required unusual strength and perseverance. They became a top crew. The team sailed the 1992 boat *America³* (USA 23) before the arrival of the *Mighty Mary* (USA 43) in time for the fourth round robin. Tactician Dave Dellenbaugh then joined the crew, the only male on board, for the final Round Robin.

Team Dennis Conner sailed the *Stars & Stripes* (USA 34), which many judges considered to be the slowest of the three 1995 defenders during the challenger series.

PACT 95 was based in Maine and led by John Marshall. The team entered the *Young America* (USA 36).

Filled with unexpected drama and excitement, the Louis Vuitton Cup series began with four round robins. During Round Robin 1 a team scored 1 point per win, 2 points per win in RR2, 4 points per win in RR3 and 5 points per win during RR4.

*One Australia* performed well until halfway through its match race of March 5, 1995 (the fourth RR), when it suddenly broke in half in heavy seas and sank within two minutes. No one was

*Part of the crew of the* Mighty Mary, *showing the determination and skill that got them to the finals of the Citizen Cup.* America[3] Foundation.

injured. AUS 35 was the first America's Cup contender ever to lose a match race by shipwreck. The AUS 31 had to be quickly made competitive. This involved casting a new 20-ton lead keel bulb for immediate delivery. The urgency was such that the casting was still so hot while being delivered, that a fire broke out on the transport vehicle between San Francisco and San Diego.

Those continuing to the semi-finals were Team New Zealand which placed first with 70 points, One Australia with 53 points, Tag Heuer Challenge with 49 points, and Nippon Challenge with 28 points.

Team New Zealand placed first in the semi-finals, winning nine of eleven races, One Australia was second, having won seven of eleven races. Tag Heuer Challenge was eliminated although they won six of eleven races. Nippon Challenge had a rough go of it and placed fourth.

*AUS 35 was the first challenger in the 144-year history of the America's Cup to ever lose a match by sinking. Fortunately, no one was injured.* www. henrythornton.com

*Team New Zealand dominated in the Louis Vuitton Cup races, becoming the official challenger for the Cup. Here* Black Magic *looks like she's about to blow over, but her team knew exactly what they were doing and prevailed.* www.americaone.org

In the finals, Team New Zealand showed how serious a contender she was by overwhelming One Australia, six races to one. Her times were significant: four minutes, fifty-five seconds; one minute, fifty-seven seconds; two minutes, twenty-six seconds, three minutes, four seconds and two minutes, thirteen seconds against one loss by fifteen seconds. The formidable *Black Magic*, NZL 32, was named the official challenger.

Similar to the Louis Vuitton Cup, the Citizen Cup was run in a series of Round Robins, with one point awarded for a win in Round Robin one, two for RR2, four for RR3 and seven for a win in RR4. *Young America* took two bonus points into the semifinals and *Stars & Stripes* took one bonus point.

Following the Round Robins, the standings were: *Young America* first with 46 points, *Stars & Stripes* second with 32 points and *America³/Mighty Mary** third with 21 points.

During the semi-finals USA 34 began taking on water and the crew put on life jackets as they feared the boat might sink. However the team, led by Dennis Conner and including Helmsman Paul Cayard, recovered and sailed well.

Then, an unusual thing happened. A compromise was reached by the three syndicates allowing all three boats to advance into the finals. *Young America* took two bonus points into the final and *Mighty Mary* took one bonus point.

The *Stars & Stripes* (USA 34) actually won the Citizen Cup with 6 points, the *Mighty Mary* and the *Young America* earning 5 points each. But, because the *Stars & Stripes* almost lost her keel during the semi-finals (she was saved by the support boats before sinking or capsizing), and judging that the yacht *Young America* was the fastest of the regatta, Team Dennis Conner petitioned and was granted the right to sail *Young America* in place of *Stars & Stripes*. Finally the defenders agreed to a compromise that in the final race, once again all three yachts would sail. The end result of

*       *Mighty Mary* replaced *America³* in Round Robin 4.

all this confusion was that Dennis Conner sailed *Young America* to defend the 1995 America's Cup against New Zealand's *Black Magic.* At this point it may be helpful to remember that part of the original Deed of Gift which basically said that any variation to the rules was acceptable as long as all participants agreed to it.

As frequently seemed to be the case, the America's Cup race itself was one-sided. New Zealand swept the event, winning five races in a row with the remarkable times of: two minutes,

*Artist's rendering of the* Mighty Mary, *almost the defending boat for the America's Cup. K. Urtz.*

*The* Stars & Stripes, *right, and the* Mighty Mary *on April 26, 1995 at the start of the final race of the Citizen Cup race.* Louis Vuitton.

*The* Young America *certainly had the most distinctive hull painting of all the yachts.* forums.hornfans.com

forty-five seconds; four minutes, fourteen seconds; one minute, fifty-one seconds; three minutes, thirty-seven seconds and one minute, fifty seconds.

The New Zealand papers referred to the match as "The Slaughter on the Water."

The New Zealand team would be a major competitor in the event in the years to come.

*The welcome given the New Zealand team when they returned home was overwhelming. And rightly so. It was only the second time in the 144-year history of the Cup that it was taken by a non-American team.* schools.natlib. govt.nz

*A proud New Zealand honored the win with a postage stamp.* www. steveirwinstamps.co.uk

# 31

# BROKEN BOATS
# AND
# A MAULED CUP

On March 14, 1996, Benjamin Peri Nathan, while chanting in Maori and wearing a Maori sovereignty T-shirt, entered the Royal New Zealand Yacht Squadron's clubroom and attacked the America's Cup trophy with a sledgehammer. The damage was so bad it was feared that the Cup could not be repaired. He was overpowered and arrested and charged with willfully damaging the cup. Pleading not guilty, Nathan used the trial to publicize his beliefs in Maori sovereignty issues. Nathan was sentenced to two years, ten months in jail; the sentence to be served in addition to an eighteen-month term he was already serving for aggravated robbery. London's Garrards silversmiths, who manufactured the cup in 1848, painstakingly restored the trophy to its original condition over a three month period, free of charge. It was flown to and from New Zealand under escort, with its own first class seat. It was again put on public view

*The Hauraki Gulf is located in New Zealand's north island, near Auckland, the largest city in that country.*
Wikimedia Foundation, Inc.

at the Royal Yacht Squadron rooms, but with increased security.

After winning the 29th America's Cup, Team New Zealand immediately accepted the challenge from the New York Yacht Club and announced the next America's Cup match would be in 2000, with the Louis Vuitton Cup being in late 1999. This delay was to avoid a conflict with the 1997/98 Whitbread Round the World Race and to give Auckland time to build the necessary infrastructure to host the cup.

First came the decision as to where to hold the event. Protected from the Pacific Ocean by islands and land masses, the Hauraki Gulf was chosen as the site of the 2000 America's Cup match and is considered ideal for racing. Because the course is so well protected, America's Cup competitors were seldom exposed to large ocean swells, but the area was known to generate a steep, punishing chop.

New Zealand, flushed with the success of *Black Magic,* offered one defender — there was no need for defender eliminations. However, the challengers came in full force to compete for the Louis Vuitton Cup. Although the New York Yacht Club was the challenger of record, by January 31, 1998 sixteen teams from ten nations had made the $US 250,000 deposit to officially challenge for the America's Cup. This was later reduced to eleven challenges from seven nations when Hong Kong, Great Britain

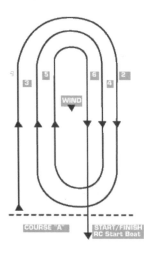

Course A, left, was the America's Cup course, a six-leg windward/leeward route measuring 18.5 nautical miles. Course B had four legs measuring 12.5 nautical miles. Course A was used in the Louis Vuitton Cup and America's Cup finals. ESPN.com

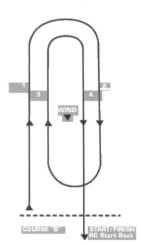

and Russia withdrew, while an American team and a French team merged into existing teams.

Sponsored by the Italian Yacht Club Punta Ala, team Prada Challenge sent a strong two-boat contingent sponsored by Prada, which became an early favorite in Auckland. The team used designer German Frers who worked for Il Moro di Venezia in 1992. Francesco de Angelis was the skipper with Rod Davis acting as the sailing coach. Team Prada acquired two boats from the America[3] syndicate for training before building ITA 45 and ITA 48.

From the St. Francis Yacht Club in San Francisco came team America One with skipper Paul Cayard. America One bought *OneAustralia* as a training boat, then developed USA 49 and USA-61 (*AmericaOne*). The team included Tactician John Kostecki and Navigator Terry Hutchinson. Cayard had an excellent yacht and put together a very professional crew, but at times his syndicate suffered from a financial hangover.

Funded by Dr. Jim Andrews, Aloha Racing, sponsored by the Waikiki Yacht Club, built on their ocean racing history to offer an America's Cup challenge from Hawaii. Skippered by veteran John Kolius, the team secured sponsorship from HealthSouth and built USA 50 and USA 54, both called *Abracadabra 2000*, and trained in Hawaii, rather than Auckland. The Hawaiian team had the most visually interesting boats. Their white yachts were airbrush sprayed

*One of the most visually dramatic boats was the Waikiki Yacht Club's*
Abracadabra 2000, *with her gleaming white hull, marine life hull paintings and*
*deep blue sails. Shown here training off Oahu.* www.wylandfoundation.org

with whales, dolphins, porpoises, a swordfish, a marlin, etc. as decorations by marine artist Wyland. Each boat side had its own design. Another eye-catching feature was the deep-blue sails.

Also from San Francisco, team America True represented the San Francisco Yacht Club. The team was led by CEO Dawn Riley (of *Mighty Mary* fame) and John Cutler served as helmsman. This team was the first to arrive in the summer of 1998/99 for training in Auckland. It was funded largely with private money provided by G. Christopher Coffin, and purchased *Tag Heuer* (NZL 39) for training before developing USA 51. The design team also benefited from America[3]'s design information. The crew included Buddy Melges and Leslie Egnot.

Spain returned with team Desafio Español sailing for the Monte Real Club de Yates de Bayona. Their team was skippered by Pedro Campos. As in 1992 and 1995, the team added Olympic medal winning sailor Luis Doreste to the crew. They were backed by the government, the Spanish royal family and major sponsor Telefonica. The team built ESP 47 designed by Rolf Vrolijk, who later worked in 2003 and 2007 as chief designer for Alinghi. Their second boat was ESP 56 which was the reconstructed and newly classified ESP 42 from 1995.

Led by experienced French campaigner Marc Pajot and with German Jochen Schumann as helmsman, the FAST 2000 team was Switzerland's first America's Cup challenge and represented Club Nautique de Morges. Their boat, the SUI 59 was an unknown quantity when she arrived in Auckland. She was certainly the most innovative entrant. Instead of a rigid single keel with a trim flap, a ballast bulb and a variable rudder, the designers installed two rotating heavy keels with bulbs of 10 tons each. Two independent helmsman had to control the yacht which made her very difficult to maneuver. Money and lack of time then prevented further technical improvement. When the mast broke during an elimination race in the Louis Vuitton Cup, the team arranged to borrow a mast from one of the Australian competitors, but this was rejected by the race committee.

*The Swiss challenger was unique with her twin keels and bulbs. Unfortunately, she was too unwieldy to be effective. K. Urtz.*

Team Le Defi Bouygues Telecom Transiciel offered a one-boat challenge from France led by Syndicate head Luc Gelluseau. Representing Union Nationale Pour La Course au Large, the team was skippered by Bertrand Pacé, who replaced Marc Pajot from the 1995 challenge, and Thierry Peponnet was the team's tactician. Their boat, (FRA 46) was considered fast and a contender. Two other French syndicates attempted to form challenges, but in the end lacked the money to compete.

The third challenge from the Japanese syndicate Nippon Challenge was funded by S&B foods chairman Tatsumitsu Yamasaki. Sponsored by the Nippon Yacht Club, the group was led by Australian Peter Gilmour. Well in advance, Japanese Professor Hideaki Myata designed fifty computer models, of which five were tank tested. The team was hit early on by the loss of former syndicate head Makoto Namba, who was lost at sea, and the Asian financial crisis, which severely limited the team's budget. It challenged with two boats, the JPN 44 and the JPN 52.

Team Dennis Conner was its namesake's ninth America's Cup competition. Referred to as Mr. America's Cup or Big Bad Dennis (depending on whether or not you are a fan), he had won the America's Cup four times, in 1974, 1980, 1987 and 1988. He has also lost it twice, in 1983 and 1995. He was, without argument, the most influential person in modern America's Cup history. Sponsored by Citizen Watches, his USA 55 adopted the name *Stars & Stripes*, common to all of Conner's boats since 1986. The team represented the San Diego Yacht Club and included Peter

*While racing the* Nippon Challenge, *the* Young America *broke in half. Although she did not sink, the effect was devastating and she was eliminated in the first round.* www.americaone.org

Isler and Ken Read in the afterguard. Peter Holmberg also joined the team as a tactician, merging the U.S. Virgin Islands Challenge into the team after that group ran out of funds.

Representing the New York Yacht Club, the challenger of record, team Young America built on John Marshall's PACT '95 syndicate. It's crew included seventeen members of various America's Cup winners. The team's yachts, USA 53* and USA 58, were designed by Bruce Farr and built on the experience gained from 1995 Cup defender *Young America.* The Helmsman was Ed Baird.

Team Young Australia was Syd Fischer's final America's Cup challenge and, as of 2014, the last America's Cup entry from Australia. The young crew was led by James Spithill, then just 19. The syndicate sailed with two old boats, *Sydney '95* (AUS 29) and *OneAustralia* (AUS 31) which were not competitive against some of the newer designs. Involved in the campaign were experienced sailors and America's Cup campaigners Sir James Hardy and Iain Murray.

The Louis Vuitton Cup consisted of three round robins (RR1-RR3). During RR1 a team scored 1 point per win. During

---

\*   In November 1999, during a race against *Nippon Challenge*, the deck of the USA 53 broke across in the middle. Both her bow and stern rose. The boat was stabilized by the auxiliary boats and did not sink. Apparently the problem was that after an earlier repair on deck the resin did not cure properly. The carbon fiber fabrics delaminated, weakening the whole construction. The team continued the competitions with USA 58, but it seemed the effect of this incident was so demoralizing they could not even reach the semifinals.

*Prada Challenge did her best against the New Zealand boat, but was swept in five races.* www.sealaunay.com

RR2 a team scored 4 points per win. During RR3 a team scored 9 points per win.

The first Round Robin races were held beginning on January 26, 2000. Six teams continued on to the semi-finals: Prada Challenge with 109 points placed first, Nippon Challenge with 102 points placed second, America True with 101 points placed third, America-One with 99 points placed fourth, Team Dennis Conner with 87 points placed fifth and Le Defi BTT with 77 points placed sixth.

The semi-finals were between teams America One which placed first with 8 points, Prada Challenge placing second with 7 points, Dennis Conner third with 7 points, Nippon Challenge placing fourth with 5 points, America True placing fifth with three points and France Le Defi BTT placing sixth with 2 points. It is

*The crew of the* Black Magic *celebrates after winning the fifth race.* news.bbc.co.uk

noteworthy that this became the first time in the history of the Cup that there was no American boat in the final race.

The final, between the two top boats in the semi's, was won by team Prada Challenge, making them the official winner of the Louis Vuitton Cup and challenger for the America's Cup.

Again the America's Cup match was swept by New Zealand. Representing the Royal New Zealand Yacht Squadron, Skipper Russell Coutts took the *Black Magic* (NZL 60) through the course beginning on February 20, 2000, winning by one minute, seven seconds; two minutes, forty-three seconds; one minute, thirty-nine seconds; one minute forty-nine seconds and forty-eight seconds.

Surprisingly, the next America's Cup would be won by a land-locked country.

*Sir Peter Blake receives the welcoming cheers of his fellow Kiwis after winning his second America's Cup.*
campsmoke.wordpress.com

*Aerial view of the crowds in Auckland after New Zealand again won the America's Cup.* Tapeka Del Mar.

# 32

# TRANSPLANTED TALENT

D uring the Twelve-Meter era, when the New York Yacht
Club still held the America's Cup, it adopted several
resolutions to strengthen nationality requirements in the
Deed of Gift. By 1980, in addition to being built in the country
of the challenger or defender, a yacht had to be designed by, and
crewed by, nationals of the country where the sponsoring yacht
club was located. However, globalization made it increasingly
impractical to enforce design nationality rules, and starting in
1984, the Royal Perth Yacht Club began relaxing this requirement. By the beginning of the 21st century the crew requirements were also relaxed. Members of the New Zealand America's Cup 2000 team became key members of the Swiss 2003
Alinghi challenge, led by biotechnology entrepreneur Ernesto
Bertarelli. To satisfy the crew nationality requirements, the New
Zealand crew became residents of Switzerland.

Once again there was no need for a defender series — New Zealand offered one defender. But the challengers swarmed Auckland. New Zealand journalist Ivor Wilkins described them as "a pack of nine hungry challengers, many of them supported by the richest men in the world and armed with transplanted New Zealand talents and their ingenuity." The New Zealand team was falling apart. More than thirty of its crew members were bought up, mostly by teams Alinghi and OneWorld.

Twenty new yachts were built, including Ilbruk Challenge, supported by the entrepreneur and off-shore sailor Michael Ilbruk. This was the first German team to enter the competition. Their challenge was later withdrawn with their GER 68 launched, but not completed.

The 2002–2003 Louis Vuitton Cup, again held in the Hauraki Gulf, saw nine teams from six countries staging 120 races over five months to select a challenger. Due to sponsorship rules, boats were not allowed to be named after their sponsors. The Oracle boat was referenced by its sail number USA 76, because the team decided not to name their boat.

The challenger of record was Italian Yacht Club Punta Ala with *Prada Challenge*. But the team that captured everyone's attention was Alinghi representing the Société Nautique de Genève, a yacht club from land-locked Switzerland. Founded by Swiss biotech billionaire Ernesto Bertarelli, Alinghi featured Russell Coutts and Brad Butterworth from Team New Zealand

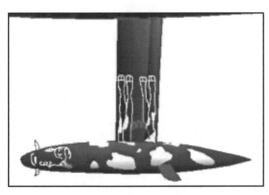

*At the "unveiling day" when all participants must show the substructure of their yachts, the Swiss painted an upsidedown cow on the keel and bulb.* K. Urtz.

and Jochen Schuemann. Their boat was SUI 64 (*Alinghi*), designed by a group which included Grant Simmer and Rolf Vrolijk. It was considered a top yacht.

From Great Britain came team GBR Challenge representing the Royal Ocean Racing Club. Put together by computer entrepreneur Peter Harrison and New Zealander David Barnes, the team was skippered by Ian Walker. They bought the JPN 44 and the JPN 52 from Nippon Challenge for study and training and hired designers Akahiro Kanai, Taro Takahashi and Derek Clark. They entered two boats, GBR 70 named the *Wight Lightning,* and GBR 78 named the *Wight Magic.*

*GBR 78 was built with a tandem keel, which was supposedly similar to the NZL 20 of 1992. She was not used in the Louis Vuitton Cup races. K. Urtz.*

France's Union Nationale Pour La Course au Large sponsored team Le Defi Areva. The French had little money and funded the first few months of their effort with the remaining budget from 2000. A sponsorship agreement with Areva, one of the world's largest civilian nuclear organizations, made it possible to take part at Auckland. But then opponents of nuclear power became involved in the form of Greenpeace and their vessel the *Rainbow Warrior.* Before the *Rainbow Warrior* was to leave as the flagship of a peace fleet aimed at preventing French nuclear tests on Mururoa atoll, she was blown up in Auckland Harbor. The ship sank and a photographer was killed. It was soon revealed that the French Intelligence Service was involved in the blast. On the first sailing day for the FRA 69, Greenpeace activists drove a motorboat into the yacht, which was damaged and took two weeks to repair. The French team then acquired the victory yacht from the 1995 America's Cup, NZL 32, as a training boat. It and

*While training in France the FRA 46 was sponsored by Monster, a French recruitment agency. On the spinnaker and the mainsail above are seen the eye-catching company logo, the "Trumpet Monster." K. Urtz.*

FRA 46 were stripped to aid in the creation of the new FRA 79. Le Defi shared the fate of many low-budget syndicates. The team arrived late in Auckland and had too little time to train there. Their boat was skippered by Luc Pillot.

Headed by shipping magnate Vincenzo Onorato, team Mascalzone Latino represented Reale Yacht Club Canottieri Savoia and featured an all-Italian crew. Paolo Ciann served as helmsman of ITA 72. The team could only finance one yacht, came late to Auckland, had no training boat and little time.

Partly financed by Microsoft mogul Paul Allen, team OneWorld was based in Seattle and carried the banner of the Seattle Yacht Club. Financing also came from Craig McCaw, who acquired his wealth through company start-ups and mergers in the mobile phone industry. Their boats, USA 65 and USA 67, were skippered by Peter Gilmour. They acquired the design team and some crew members from Team New Zealand, including chief designer Laurie Davidson. During the Louis Vuitton match, team Dennis Conner and team Prada tried to have OneWorld disqualified because it had received technical information from team New Zealand. The America's Cup Arbitration Panel fined OneWorld $65,000 and docked

 *ITA 80's spoon bow, right, upset owner Patrizio Bertelli. All the other boats had adopted the double kink bow from the previous Cup winner, NZL 60, left.* K. Urtz.

them one Louis Vuitton point for each subsequent race for this infraction.

Team Oracle BMW Racing sailed for the Golden Gate Yacht Club of San Francisco. Larry Ellison, owner of the software company, is one of the richest men in the world and a passionate and successful sailor in ocean going yachts. He bought and built on the assets of the 2000 syndicate AmericaOne. The Oracle BMW Racing team was skippered by Peter Holmberg and included Paul Cayard, Chris Dickson and members of seven earlier syndicates. Their boats, USA 71 and USA 76, were designed by Bruce Farr.

The team Prada Challenge had a crew which included members of the 2000 Young America syndicate. They were again skippered by Francesco de Angelis and Rod Davis was in the afterguard. A lot of media attention focused on a dispute about the bow section between owner Patrizio Bertelli and the chief designer Doug Peterson (who designed the 1992 champion USA 23). While all the other teams had adopted the double-kink-bow of the previous America's Cup winner NZL 60, Peterson designed a spoon bow. The result was that he left Prada. The bow section was then cut off and replaced three times during the last LVC Rounds.

Once more into the fray was Dennis Conner. He hired the Reichel Plug group as designers and Ken Read as skipper. Their main boat, USA 77, sank in fifty feet of water off the California coast in July before the Cup began. The yacht was raised and repaired immediately. Critics classified it as worthless. Due to a small budget, the team trained only a short time in New Zealand. Conner also had USA 66.

Sweden's yacht club, Gamla Stans Yacht Sallskap, offered team Victory Challenge with the boats SWE 63 and SWE 73 skippered by Mats Johansson. The project was funded by Jan Stenbeck, owner of TV2, TV3 and Europe's first free newspaper *Metro*. He then acquired NZL 38, sister ship of the 1995 America's Cup winner, for study and training. The boat was carefully overhauled and renamed "Christiana." From Prada he hired the designer German (Mani) Frers, successful son of the well-known German Frers. The resultant boat, SWE 63 was often referred to as a NZL 60 derivative. The crew included the best sailors in Scandinavia. Shortly after the christening of SWE 63 and six weeks before the start of the Louis Vuitton Cup match, Stenbek died of a heart attack. The team continued in his memory. This was Sweden's first America's Cup bid since 1992.

The Louis Vuitton Cup races were held from October 1, 2002 to January 19, 2003. Somewhat confusing was the addition of a repêchage round. This was an additional race which allowed teams finishing round robins just below the top four, a chance to advance to the quarter-final stage. Thus the races consisted of two Round Robins followed by quarter-finals with two repêchage rounds, semi-finals with one repêchage round and finals. The end result was they had no effect. *Alinghi* and Oracle BMW Racing, who placed first and second in the Round Robins, faced each other in the final. *Alinghi* won 5 to 1 and was named the official challenger.

Although the America's Cup match was another sweep, this time it was New Zealand that lost five races in succession.

The first race was on February 15, 2003. Team New Zealand started with a slight advantage after an even start, but was soon plagued by seas coming over the side and the cockpit flooding. The added weight of sea water led to the boom breaking and the headsail tack ring pulling out. New Zealand had to withdraw. The score was *Alinghi* 1, New Zealand 0.

The second race took place the following day. *Alinghi* led after the upwind leg, but was passed on the first downwind run and trailed for most of the race. Superior speed and better tactics on

*In the first race Team New Zealand had more than its share of mishaps. Here water can be seen coming in over the rail and accumulating inside the boat along the after starboard side.* Ivor Wilkins.

*Team New Zealand lost the second race by a mere seven seconds, the fourth closest race in America's Cup history. Returning to port, the team is exhausted and downhearted.* Stephanie LAMY/DPPI.

the final run allowed *Alinghi* to pass just before the finish. Team New Zealand lost by a heartbreaking seven seconds.

During the third race on February 18, *Alinghi* benefited from a shift to the right to take the lead. Team New Zealand was able to close the gap, but never managed to pass. *Alinghi* won by 23 seconds. The score was now *Alinghi* 3, Team New Zealand 0.

After waiting over one week for suitable weather, the fourth race got underway on February 28. *Alinghi* hit the start line first, and with good speed and a slight left shift, was able to cross and lead for the first upwind and downwind leg. On the second lap, Team New Zealand trailed by three boat lengths. She then suffered

*Above,* Alinghi *leads Team New Zealand around a turn in the fourth race. The New Zealand boat then lost her mast, below, and had to withdraw.* Daniel Forster.

a fatal mast failure, possibly from pushing the boat too hard, and was forced to withdraw.

In the fifth race, held on March 2, *Alinghi* lead from start to finish. She had a slight advantage at the beginning and showed superior speed and tactics throughout, to complete a 5-0 sweep

*Above, the* Alinghi *crew celebrate their win. Below, skipper Russell Coutts hoists the trophy aloft.* Above, Daniel Forster, below, Max Ranchi.

over Team New Zealand. The Cup returned to Europe for the first time in 155 years.

# 33

# ACT I, SCENE I ...

For the 2007 Cup, Ernesto Bertarelli's Société Nautique de Genève (SNG) rescinded all interpretive resolutions to the deed, essentially leaving "constructed in country" as the only remaining nationality requirement. The 2007 defense of the Cup was held in Valencia, Spain. This was the first time since the original 1851 Isle of Wight race that the America's Cup match was held in Europe, or in a country different from that of the defender (necessary because Switzerland does not border a "sea or arm of the sea" as specified in the deed). Eleven challenging yacht clubs from nine countries submitted formal entries in a sport that required funding of at least $50 million per team to be competitive.

Two significant changes had occurred since 2003. First, in 2003 SUI 64 (*Alinghi*) had cut the top of its mainsail creating more sail area, thus taking advantage of the faster winds higher off the water. By 2007 all teams followed this design with a horizontal

*The top of* Alinghi*'s mainsail, which was the only one of its kind in 2003, was duplicated by every other boat entered in the 2007 Cup match. The concept was that by lopping off the tip of the sail, more surface was available to catch upper winds. K. Urtz.*

upper edge to the mainsail.

Second, Ernesto Bertarelli took over management of the Louis Vuitton Cup match series and the rules were completely changed. The Repêchage Rounds were eliminated. A new protocol was introduced consisting of thirteen events called "Acts." The Acts with odd numbers were fleet-races with each boat sailing for points. The Acts with the even numbers were match races with one team sailing against another. In a complicated points system, some points collected in the Acts were counted toward the Round Robins. A total of 566 races (according to one source) were held at Marseilles; Naples; Malmö, Sweden; Trapani, Italy and Valencia, Spain, beginning in September 2004.

The actual challenger selection series, the Louis Vuitton Cup 2007, ran from April 16 to June 6, 2007 and consisted of two round robins, two semi-finals and a final.

BMW Oracle, from the United States, was the Challenger of Record. Their sponsoring club was San Francisco's Golden Gate Yacht Club. BMW Oracle entered two boats: USA 87 and

*USA 98 during Race 1 of the semi-finals on May 14, 2007.* Reuters.

USA 98. Larry Ellison owner of Oracle, led Skipper Chris Dickson, both of whom were also listed as helmsmen. Their design team was Bertrand Pacé. The afterguard included John Kostecki and Eric Doyle. Because of the strong financial and technical participation of the car company, the team had been renamed from Oracle BMW to BMW Oracle. When USA 76 was damaged in an overnight storm in Valencia, the team continued training with the old USA 71 until a second training yacht, USA 81, and the racing boat USA 87 were completed. This was followed by USA 98.

Once the events of 2003 were over, Patricio Bertelli announced he was through with ocean racing. He later changed his mind, regrouped with financial backing from Telecom Italia (TIM), and entered the 2007 challenge. His sponsoring club in Italy was the Yacht Club Italiano. His syndicate was Luna Rossa Challenge. Their team included Skipper/Helmsman Francesco de Angelis and helmsman James Spithill. Training began with 2003 veterans ITA 74 and ITA 86 but their competition boat was ITA 94 (*Luna Rossa*).

Spain was represented by the syndicate Desfío Español 2007. At first unable to decide on Barcelona or Valencia for a yacht club to sponsor them, they finally chose the Spanish Sailing Federation (Real Federación Española de Vela). Although it was not a yacht club, there

The ITA 94 *(*Luna Rossa*) in the Louis Vuitton Cup final of 2007.* pinterest.com

*On February 10, 2007 the Swedish challenger, SWE 96, was launched with the traditional breaking of a bottle of champagne on the bow by Kristina Anker of the Victory Challenge team.* Victory Challenge.

were no protests, so it was allowed. Most of their funding came from Iberdrola, a financially strong energy group. The Spanish team was lead by Agustin Zulueta with Luis Doreste serving as skipper and Karol Jablonski as helmsman. The Spanish boat was ESP 97.

The family of the late Jan Stenbeck of Sweden, had difficulty with financing until Red Bull, a first time America's Cup corporate sponsor, came on board. This enabled them to build a new yacht, the SWE 96 *Järv* (Wolverine). They represented the yacht club Gamla Stans Yacht Sällskap. Their syndicate was Victory Challenge led by Hugo Stenbeck. Their boat was designed by German (Mani) Frers. The skipper and helmsman was Magnus Holmberg. The afterguard included Johan Barne and Mattias Rahm.

Also returning from Italy was the Mascalzone Latino Team Capitalia. Vincenzo Onorato and his team represented the Reale Yacht Club Canottieri Savoia. Their boats were designed by Harry

*The strikingly colorful Republic of South Africa's RSA 83 working in the Louis Vuitton Cup races. www.kerdesign.com*

Dunning, Reichel and Pugh. Skipper Vasco Vascotto at first trained on USA 76 and USA 77 purchased from Dennis Conner. Once racing began, they used ITA 99.

New to the America's Cup was the Republic of South Africa. Their Team Shosholoza (meaning "Go Forward" and the title of a song sung at sporting events and popular with South African miners) represented the Royal Cape Yacht Club. Syndicate head Capt. Salvatore Sarno, South Africa Manager of the Mediterranean Shipping Company in Durban, sailed with a mixed crew to demonstrate the end of apartheid. Their training boat, the ITA 48, and sister ship of the LVC 2000 winner ITA 45, was rumored to have cost €525,000. Once Louis Vuitton racing began they used the new RSA 83, the first IACC yacht built by the new Version 5* rule.

From France came the syndicate K-Challenge Areva Challenge, sponsored by the yacht club Cercle de la Voile de Paris. Headed by Stephane Kandler, the team included skipper Dawn Riley and helmsmen Thierry Peponnet and Sebastian Col. For training boats, Kandler was able to lease the AC 2000 winner NZL 60 and her sister the NZL 57. The team's designers were D. Nicolopoulos and B. Nivet. Following Acts 1-3 of the early Louis Vuitton series, he paired with German sailing ace Jochen Schuemann,

---

\*   Version 5.0 of the International America's Cup Class Rule was issued on December 15, 2003. Specifics were: length: 25 meters (82 ft.), weight: 24 tonnes (24 long tons; 26 short tons), height of the mast: 35 meters (115 ft.), weight of the bulb: 19 tonnes (19 long tons; 21 short tons), sail surface area: 325 square meters (389 sq. yd.) upwind, 750 square meters (900 sq. yd.) downwind, crew: 17+ "18th man."

*The +39 (ITA 85) on her first test sailing in Valencia on October 20, 2006. +39 Challenge.*

changed the syndicate name to Areva Challenge, shifted his yacht club to Union Nationale pour la Course au Large and competed in the remainder of the Louis Vuitton races with the FRA 93.

The third contender from Italy was the syndicate +39 Challenge (+39 is the telephone country code for Italy and became the name of the team's racing boat). Sailing for the Circolo Vela Gargnano Yacht Club, they were headed-by Lorenzo Rizzardi with Luca Devoti as skipper, Giovanni Ciccarelli as designer and Iain Percy as helmsman. For training purposes they bought SUI 59 (the former Be Happy/FAST 2000) from Alinghi. Their competition boat was the new Version5 yacht, the ITA 85.

After years of failed attempts, Germany succeeded in putting together the right combination of yacht club, financial backing, design team and boat racing prowess to challenge in 2007. CEO Uwe Sasse headed the syndicate United Internet Team Germany, representing the Deutscher Challenger Yacht Club. For training boats they first acquired the earlier contender, ITA 72, which was operating on Lake Constance. As a second training boat they acquired Alinghi's SUI 91. Their final racing boat, the V5 type GER 89, was drawn by designer Michel Richardson and built by Knieriem Jachtbau of Kiel.

Another first time entrant came from China. While well-funded and having excellent organizational skills, they were short

*The Chinese entry was noteworthy for its bright yellow hull and red, fire-breathing dragon. Unfortunately they had only one win against nineteen loses.*
iacc120cup.altervista.org

in experience. Syndicate China Team CEO Chaoyong Wang was chairman of the China Equity Investment Group, a leading Chinese venture capital firm, and formerly head of Morgan Stanley, Beijing. His co-investor and Project Advisor was Yifei Li, a martial arts champion and managing director of MTV China. Their team also included Co-Executive Director Xavier de Lesquen, Co-Director Pierre Mas, General Coordinator Luc Gellusseau and Project advisor Nicolas Ajacques. For training purposes they acquired FRA 69 and FRA 79. The first one was then dismantled and part of the hardware was used on the CHN 95, their challenger in the Louis Vuitton Cup.

The 2007 Louis Vuitton Cup was held in Valencia, Spain, from April 16 to June 6. The standings after the Round Robins are shown in the chart on the following page. The top four boats went on to the semi-finals, while the remainder were eliminated. By placing first, Emirates Team New Zealand was then allowed to choose who it wished to compete against. They chose the Spanish boat and, predictably beat them, five to two. The other semi-final race was won by Luna Rossa Challenge, upsetting favorite BMW Oracle Racing by five to one. The finals were taken in five straight races, with Emirates Team New Zealand then becoming

| LOUIS VUITTON CUP | | Bonus Points | Round Robin 1 | Round Robin 2 | Total | Ranking |
|---|---|---|---|---|---|---|
| Emirates Team New Zealand | NZL 92 | 4 | | | 4 | 1 |
| BMW Oracle Racing | USA 98 | 3 | | | 3 | 2 |
| Luna Rossa Challenge | ITA 94 | 3 | | | 3 | 2 |
| Desafio Español 2007 | ESP 97 | 3 | | | 3 | 2 |
| Mascalzone Latino - Capitalia Team | ITA 99 | 2 | | | 2 | 5 |
| Victory Challenge | SWE 96 | 2 | | | 2 | 5 |
| Team Shosholoza | RSA 83 | 2 | | | 2 | 5 |
| +39 Challenge | ITA 85 | 2 | | | 2 | 5 |
| Areva Challenge | FRA 93 | 1 | | | 1 | 9 |
| United Internet Team Germany | GER 89 | 1 | | | 1 | 9 |
| China Team | CHN 95 | 1 | | | 1 | 9 |

the official challenger for the America's Cup.

Valencia, Spain was chosen as the site for the America's Cup because the Alinghi syndicate put the hosting rights out for competitive bid. In the first round, the bids of Barcelona, Palma de Mallorca, Porto Cervo and Elba were eliminated. The four finalists were Cascais (near Lisbon), Marseille, Naples and Valencia. On November 27, 2003 it was announced that the venue would be Valencia, Spain. A new building, Veles e Vents designed by David Chipperfield, was built in the harbour of Valencia to house the central base for all the America's Cup teams.

All the races were run on a windward-leeward course consisting of four legs with legs 1 and 4 being 3.3 nautical miles (6.1 km.) in length, and legs 2 and 3 being 3.0 nautical miles (5.6 km.) for a total of 12.6 nautical miles (23.3 km.). As it was decided there was an advantage to the team that started from the right side of the course, a coin toss placed Emirates Team New Zealand there for the first race. Each team would alternate sides

Alinghi *(left) and Emirates Team New Zealand in race one of the thirty-second America's Cup.* freshwater2006

*In the third race a small rip developed in the New Zealand spinnaker (left) which then blew apart. A second spinnaker was hoisted before being properly attached and blew like a flag from the mast head. Note also sail dragging off the starboard side. The third spinnaker worked after four minutes of chaos but* Alinghi *was then in the lead.* Associated Press.

in subsequent starts.

The *Alinghi* won the first race by thirty-five seconds in 12-knot winds. The second race was won by Emirates Team New Zealand by twenty-eight seconds. They also took the third race by twenty-five seconds and it was beginning to look like New Zealand would make a comeback. But then the *Alinghi* took the fourth race and it was all tied up. From then on it was *Alinghi*'s match. She won races 5, 6 and 7 by nineteen seconds, twenty-eight seconds and one second, respectively. *Alinghi* retained the Cup.

It is interesting to note that of the crew on the Swiss boat, Ernesto Bertarelli was the only Swiss on board, while on the Emirates boat there were fourteen New Zealand residents in the crew.

The next America's Cup, in 2010, would be entirely different, both in presentation and outcome.

# 34

# COURTING VICTORY

F ollowing its successful defense of the Cup on July 3, 2007, Société Nautique de Genève* (SNG) accepted a challenge for the 33rd America's Cup from Club Náutico Español de Vela (CNEV), a newly formed yacht club, created for the purpose of challenging for the Cup. CNEV had no boats, no clubhouse, only four members (vice presidents of the Spanish Sailing Federation), and had never run a regatta of any type. On July 5, 2007 SNG and CNEV released the protocol for the next Cup match. The protocol was heavily criticized, with some teams and yacht clubs calling it the worst in the history of the event.

The Golden Gate Yacht Club** (GGYC) initiated legal action against SNG in the New York Supreme Court alleging violations of the Deed of Gift of the America's Cup. (New York courts decide disputes regarding the terms of the Deed of Gift

---
\*     Representing Ernesto Bertarelli and team Alinghi.
\*\*    Representing Larry Ellison and team BMW Oracle.

because the America's Cup is held under the terms of a charitable legal trust established under New York law). The suit alleged that CNEV did not meet the terms of the Deed of Gift as a legitimate yacht club because it never held an annual regatta, a requirement under the Deed of Gift. At the same time, GGYC issued a challenge for the Cup.

Because of the precedent set in the 1988 America's Cup when the San Diego Yacht Club defended against a monohull yacht with a catamaran, any non mutual-consent challenger must specify the largest multi-hull possible under the terms of the Deed of Gift. Consequently, GGYC specified its yacht as having a 90-foot waterline, and 90-foot beam. However, GGYC also asked for "consensual negotiations in the spirit of the Deed of Gift toward a Protocol comparable in scope, and similar in terms, to that used for the 32nd America's Cup." But despite extensive negotiations and proposals made by both sides, GGYC and SNG were unable to agree upon a mutual consent Protocol.

On November 27, 2007 the court ruled in favor of GGYC. It stated that CNEV was not a valid challenger, and declared GGYC the proper and legal challenger. SNG was instructed to meet GGYC's challenge under Deed of Gift terms unless they could agree on other terms by mutual consent.

This lead to more than two years of legal action from both sides. Everything was in dispute, including: the meaning of "having for its annual regatta," as used in the Deed of Gift; when entries could be accepted; holding a multi-challenger match or not; when to hold the races; which hemisphere they would be held in, whether or not Al Hamra Village in the Ras al-Khaimah emirate of the United Arab Emirates was a Deed Legal Venue; the legality of building a boat with powered winches and moveable ballast; the filing of a Custom House Certificate within fourteen days of the event; measurement procedures for the yachts; the use of a friction-reduction system that involved discharging liquids in the sea; the meaning of "constructed in country" as applied to boats in the Deed of Gift, and multitude of other points.

Several organizations submitted *amicus curiae* (friend of the court) briefs. In particular, on December 31, 2008, the New York Yacht Club (NYYC), the oldest and longest holder of the America's Cup, filed a brief supporting GGYC's position.

*The BMW Oracle Racing America's Cup yacht* USA 17 *sailing off of Valencia, Spain on January 22, 2010.* CC BY-SA 3.0view.

The result of all this was that because the two parties were unable to agree otherwise, the 2010 America's Cup match took place in Valencia, Spain, as a one-on-one Deed of Gift match in gigantic, specialized multi-hull racing yachts with no other clubs or teams participating.

BMW Oracle Racing launched a 90-foot (27 m.) trimaran on August 2008 in Anacortes, Washington. After three weeks of shakedown cruises, the boat was shipped to San Diego,

*The* Alinghi 5 *practicing before the America's Cup match in Valencia.* karsten. heimberger-net.de

California where it underwent fourteen months of development. During this time the boat was extensively modified, most notably in replacing the outer floats, adding powered hydraulics, and fitting a rigid wing sail. At the end of December 2009, the boat was shipped to Valencia, where it arrived on January 4, 2010. Initially known as *BMW Oracle Racing 90* (BOR90), the yacht was renamed *USA 17* to conform with the notice of challenge when launched in Valencia.

Team Alinghi built a catamaran at a boatyard in Villeneuve, Switzerland, named *Alinghi 5* which was 90-foot (27 m.) on the waterline with a bowsprit that made her "about 120-foot (37 m.) overall." Somewhat controversially, team Alinghi installed an engine to power the hydraulics. The boat was launched on July 8, 2009, being lifted from a construction shed in Villeneuve by a Mil Mi-26 helicopter and carried to Lake Geneva. On August 7, 2009, the same type of helicopter moved the boat from Lake Geneva to Genoa, Italy. At the end of September 2009, the boat was shipped to Ras al Khaimah. At the end of December 2009, the boat was shipped to Valencia, where it arrived on January 5, 2010.

*Looking like a water bug skittering across a pond, the* USA 17 *races across the water. Note how the crew seem to be dwarfed by the size of the boat.* www.strangeracer.com

The first race took place on February 12 in 5-10 knot winds. An aggressive pre-start by team BMW Oracle Racing forced a foul by team Alinghi. Both boats wound up headed into the wind over the start line. Team Alinghi bore off while team BMW Oracle Racing remained stalled and started about 650 meters behind but was clearly able to sail higher (closer to the wind) and faster (average speed 20.2 knots vs. 19.4 knots), so they caught up with the *Alinghi 5* within fifteen minutes and extended their lead, eventually winning by over 3,000 meters. Upwind they were able to out-sail team Alinghi even without a jib and their speed differential was greater downwind (23.5 knots vs. 20.7 knots average speed) than upwind. The final time of fifteen minutes, twenty-eight seconds included a penalty turn by team Alinghi due to not keeping clear at the start.

The second race was held two days later in 7-8 knot winds. Team Alinghi received a penalty for being in the pre-start area before the designated time. There was very little pre-start maneuvering. The USA 17 started on a port tack ahead of team Alinghi on a starboard tack. Team Alinghi sailed faster than

*Alinghi 5 (foreground) and USA 17 square off during race one for the America's Cup. Note how little of the hulls of each boat is in the water.* www.cupinfo. com

*Larry Ellison proudly holds the America's Cup over his head after winning it in a long legal, and short sporting, battle.* www.businessweek.com

during the previous race and benefited from a 20-degree wind shift, which put the Swiss boat in the lead at about the midpoint of the first leg. But after crossing ahead, they tacked and fell behind. Team BMW Oracle Racing then proved to be much faster on the first reach, pulling about 2 kilometers ahead (26.8 knots vs. 25.2 knots average speed), winning by five minutes, twenty-six seconds. The final time includes the penalty turn by Alinghi.

BMW Oracle Racing had won the America's Cup.

This match was responsible for two major changes in America's Cup racing. First, the transition to multi-hulls proved something that power boat racers had known for a long time: the less hull that is used to displace water, the faster the boat goes. Put another way, if you minimize the amount of friction or drag between the hull and the water, the boat will go faster. The speed and design of multi-hulls did just that — reduced the drag of the hull through the water by bringing it out of the water. Second, after its win in the first race, most observers realized the rigid wing sail gave the USA 17 a decisive advantage. Multi-hulls and rigid wing sails would be state-of-the-art, the wave of the future (pun intended) in America's Cup events.

---

TRAVELING WITH THE AMERICA'S CUP TROPHY

Following the win in Valencia, Elizabeth Murphy, Oracle's executive producer of special events and programs, was appointed "Trophy Wife" to the Cup. As such, part of her duties include accompanying the trophy everywhere. This involves a lot of air travel which required that Murphy study aircraft configurations — the Cup doesn't fit in a standard first-class seat. She knows customs requirements for every country, and knows a lot about security. While traveling, the trophy is never left alone and requires two full-time security guards. When asked what is in the Louis Vuitton trunk, Murphy sometimes quips, "My ex-husband."

Elizabeth Murphy considers her Trophy Wife role as a great privilege, "Men, women and children seem to have a love affair with her. Sometimes, when we are flying for twelve hours and I'm sitting next to her, I think of where she has been and who she has met and how profound it is that some of the most powerful men in the world have spent what could be billions of dollars (collectively) to win her."

*Elizabeth Murphy, the "trophy wife," with the Cup.* San Francisco Chronicle.

# PART II

# AMERICA'S CUP IN SAN FRANCISCO

# 35

# AMERICA'S CUP 2013

At the time of Team Oracle's victory in February 2010, the global economy was on a multi-year-long downward slide. Whether it would improve or continue declining was anyone's guess. Unfortunately, as time passed the economy worsened, with dramatic, and unforeseen effects on America's Cup 2013.

Team Oracle's victory at Valencia marked the beginning of a new era. The existing ACC (America's Cup Class) was becoming outdated. The monohulls with their heavy keels and soft sails had reached and passed their peak. The public was losing interest. It was time for a new class of racing yacht; something faster, more exciting, something to capture and hold the viewing audience. And, of course, the larger the audience, the more sponsors' products would be purchased.

The answer was multihulls. In June 2010 Morrelli & Melvin Design and Engineering, and U.S. Sailing were asked, by Russell Coutts representing BMW Oracle, to work up options for a new class of multihull yacht. They were told the design should be uniform in the sense that it would ensure close racing in a wide range of wind conditions. The number of hulls, masts appendages and sails would be limited to minimize costs. The boat should be capable of being shipped by air and soft sails would be eliminated in favor of a wingsail, which gave the boats enough power to foil out of the water even in light winds.

This resulted in a multihulled boat that could race in winds between 5 and 30 knots, equipped with a wingsail and soft sails for downwind sailing. The boat could be taken apart and transported by air, ready to ship in 24 hours and able to sail again within 48 hours of arrival. To keep the human aspect in the competition the hydraulics that controlled the wings were pressurized by crew members grinding on winches, as opposed to replacing the men with machinery.

The new rules and details of the next America's Cup were announced in September 2010 in Valencia, Spain. At that time discussions were ongoing with San Francisco to host the racing, but not yet confirmed. The venue was scheduled to be announced by December 31, 2010.

The boats and the racing schedule were unprecedented, innovative, and designed to regenerate public enthusiasm, encourage young sailors to become interested in the sport and give the sailing crews a bold leap into a new, adventurous era.

First, the only boats allowed to race would be catamarans. These would conform to the design rule for the AC (America's Cup) 72. This was a 72-foot-long catamaran with a hard wingsail 131 feet tall, replacing fabric mainsails. The boat would be 46 feet wide and weigh 15,000 pounds. Each team would be allowed to build two boats.

Second, to help shore crews and sailors adjust to the new technology and multihulls, a series of races would begin in 2011

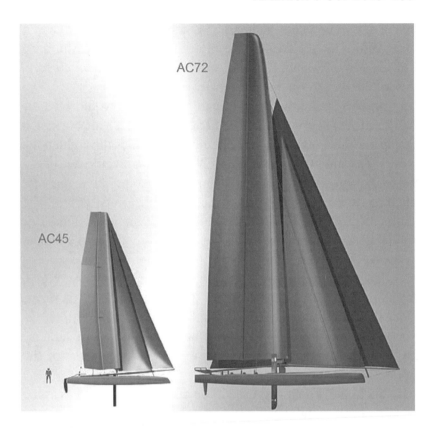

*Above, relative sizes of the proposed AC catamarans, compared to a human (lower left). The center downward projection on each boat is a daggerboard, not a keel or rudder. Below, proposed statistics for the two boats.* Image, 2010 America's Cup Organizers, statistics, 2012 cupinfo.com

**Approximate Dimensions**

|  | AC72 | AC45 |
|---|---|---|
| Length Over All : | 72 ft | 44.13 ft |
| Beam : | 46 ft | 22.6 ft |
| Draft : | 14 ft 5 in | |
| Mast Height : | 131 ft 7 in | 70 ft 6 in |
| Displacement : | 12,555 - 13,007 lbs | 3086 lbs |
| Sail area : | | |
| Wing only | 2744 - 2798 sq ft | 915 sq ft |
| Gennaker | 3444 sq ft (Estimated) | 515 sq ft AC72 |
| Main & Gennaker | 6242 sq ft (Estimated) | 1430 sq ft |

with a new one-design catamaran, 45 feet long, also with a wing-sail. Known as the AC45, it would come from Core Builders, Ltd., in New Zealand, with the only variations being allowed in the soft sails and some of the hardware components.

As to scheduling, in 2011 and 2012 teams would race the AC45s in the America's Cup World Series (ACWS), in both match racing and fleet racing, to be held in various cities throughout the world. The intent was that the ACWS regattas would help publicize the upcoming America's Cup, increase public awareness of the new boats and their abilities, and bring visibility to the teams as they sought sponsors. Any team, whether defender or challenger for the final America's Cup, was required to compete in the ACWS series.

The first generation of AC72s would race in the ACWS in the summer of 2012, a year before the Louis Vuitton Cup races. Once this happened, the AC45s would be used for a youth series. Second generation AC72s would begin launching in January 2013, allowing six months preparation before the start of the Louis Vuitton series.

Yacht hulls were required to be built in the sponsor's home country, other components could be made elsewhere. There were no nationality requirements as to sailors and designers.

Although full details were not disclosed, organizers said that race oversight and event operation would be by independent bodies to assure a fair and neutral treatment of all participants.

The agenda also included creating ambitious upgrades to broadcast technology and Internet accessibility. Races would be shorter and less subject to wind delays.

Russell Coutts: "During our six months of planning we spoke to the teams, to commercial partners, to media and to the fans. A clear and compelling vision emerged — that to capture and communicate the excitement our sport can produce, we need the best sailors racing the fastest boat in the world."

Limits were placed on the number of boats, rudders and daggerboards to control costs. Likewise, there were restrictions on the number of support boats, and no-sail periods were instituted. The onboard crew of the AC72s was limited to eleven. The thrust of this was cost control. Not that the organizers expected to create draconian spending limits, rather, their aim was simply to keep spending from getting out of reach too quickly.

In September 2010 the dates for the 2013 America's Cup were announced. The Louis Vuitton Cup would be held in July 2013. The first AC72s would be launched in November 2011. They would race in the ACWS in San Francisco in December 2012.

The Challenger of Record, Club Nautica di Roma, had been accepted immediately after BMW Oracle's 2010 Victory. Now it was announced that additional challengers would be accepted as of November 1, 2010.

New Zealand jumped the gun. Their email challenge was received at the Golden Gate Yacht Club one second before midnight on October 31 and was rejected for being too early. A challenge from Artemis Racing arrived fifteen seconds after midnight, making them the first of the multiple challengers to file. New Zealand then re-filed forty-nine minutes later.

An early challenge deadline was set for March 31, 2011. Subsequent challenges would be accepted only at the discretion of the Golden Gate Yacht Club (GGYC). There were eleven challengers on file by the March deadline. As the GGYC had a

*Team Artemis Racing shortly after announcing their challenge for the America's Cup.* sailingsweden.se

policy of not publicly announcing challengers; it was up to the challenging sponsor to do so if it wished. In December the French team, Aleph-Équipe De France and the Multihull Yacht Club of Queensland, Australia filed challenges. January 2012 brought a challenge from another French team, the Peyron brothers and their Energy Team. In March came challenges from China, Korea, Italy and three unnamed teams.

Later the Australian team dropped out due to funding difficulties. Then, in May, the Challenger of Record (COR), representing Club Nautico di Roma, withdrew. The role of COR then went to the second challenger, Sweden's Artemis Racing. With it came the right to veto any change in the Protocol, even if the other challengers agreed otherwise.

On June 15, 2011 the official list of challengers was announced:

| COUNTRY | TEAM | SPONSORING CLUB |
|---------|------|-----------------|
| China | China Team | Mei Fan Yacht Club |
| France | Aleph-Équipe De France | Aleph Yacht Club |
| France | Energy Team | Yacht Club of France |
| Italy | Venezia Challenge | Club Canottieri di Lauria |
| New Zealand | Emirates Team New Zealand | Royal New Zealand YS |
| Rep. of Korea | Team Korea | Sail Korea Yacht Club |
| Spain | GreenComm | Real Club Nautico de Valencia |
| Sweden | Artemis Racing | Kungliga Svenska Segel Sallskapet |

In addition to Australia, the list of those withdrawing later included Canada, Italy, France and Russia, all due to the difficulty in raising funds.

In early June 2011, trying to make it easier on would-be challengers, the America's Cup organizers moved the earliest launch dates for the AC72s back six months to July 2012. They also waived the requirements for the $1.5 million performance bond and the one million euro entry fee, replacing them with a simple $100,000 entry fee. The greatest hurdle was then the requirement to buy an AC45 and race it in the ACWS, an investment estimated at $1.5 million per boat, plus the cost of personnel at each port the boat raced in.

The above concessions were in addition to the Shared Design Program, which had been announced in April. This program allowed any of the challengers and the defender to take part in a common study of the hull, wingsail and appendage designs needed to produce a basic AC72. The hull would be designed by Van Peteghem Lauriot Prevost of France, and the wingsail and soft sails by North Technology Groups, each an industry leader in its field. This basic AC72 would then be used as a foundation for their team's final racing yacht. What would have been against the rules in earlier years (knowing the configuration of your opponent's boat) was now encouraged (within limits). The thrust of the program was to get a technically advanced and new yacht class developed in a shortened time frame.

The challenger roster increased in October 2011 when the GGYC accepted Patrizio Bertelli and Team Prada of Italy. They had negotiated a shared design agreement with Emirates Team New Zealand to share design information and testing results, providing the boat itself was built in Italy.

There were additional challenger dropouts in early 2012. Aleph pulled out in April due to an inability to meet funding goals. Hugues Lepic, chairman: "… the economic environment does not allow us to go all the way to San Francisco in 2013."

That same month, GreenComm of Spain withdrew, unable to generate enough funds.

Although China competed all the way through the ACWS series, they did not pay their entry fee for the Cup races and were dropped.

The biggest disappointment in the diminishing ranks of challengers was the loss of the Peyron brothers of France and their Energy Team. They announced on August 1, 2012 that they did not have the funding necessary to build a new AC72, but would continue competing in the ACWS and enter a Youth

*Shown training for an America's Cup World Series race in Plymouth, England, the Aleph Yacht Club team of France later had to withdraw because of funding problems.* Pierrick Contin

Series team also, with the goal of becoming a challenger for the next America's Cup.

Korea also made a valiant try, but in March 2013 confirmed they were withdrawing. They withdrew from the ACWS series a month later.

In the end, seven AC72s would be built: one for Luna Rossa Challenge and two apiece for Artemis Racing, Emirates Team New Zealand and Oracle Team USA.

The global economy, who knew?

# 36

# FRONT ROW, CENTER

The S.S. *Jeremiah O'Brien* is an operating museum ship berthed at pier 45 in San Francisco's Fisherman's Wharf area. She is one of the 2,710 Liberty ships built by the United States Maritime Commission (now the Maritime Administration) during World War II. She is also one of the two operating Liberty ships remaining in the United States,* and the only one in the world in her original configuration.

Most Liberty ships were built as freighters, designed to carry the necessary tanks, trucks, jeeps, ambulances, food, weapons, ammunition, and countless other items necessary for our troops in Europe, the South Pacific and the Far East. Some Liberty ships were built, on the same hull design, as tankers, hospital ships, troop ships and to transport aircraft. Unless they were

---

\* The other is the S.S. *John W. Brown*, located in Baltimore, Maryland.

transferred to a branch of the armed services, all Liberty ships were managed by commercial (civilian) steamship companies and operated by civilian merchant mariners. They were armed with either a 3-inch gun or a 5-inch gun at each end and carried eight or more anti-aircraft machine guns mounted on the main deck and superstructure. A U.S. Navy group, known as the Armed Guard, manned the weapons. There were twelve or more men in each Armed Guard, depending on when the ship was launched (because the war escalated so quickly, the Navy at times had difficulty recruiting and training enough personnel) and the ship's purpose (troopships carried a larger contingent than freighters).

First time visitors often assume that because the ship is painted grey and has guns it is a Navy ship. Their first question is usually, "When was she commissioned?"

The answer is, she was never commissioned, she was christened and launched. She is a merchant ship, not a Navy ship. Only Navy ships are commissioned.

The S.S. *Jeremiah O'Brien* was launched in 1943 at South Portland, Maine. She was named after the man who fought and won the first naval battle of the Revolutionary War. Operating for Grace Line, she made seven wartime voyages between her launching and the end of the war. The first four voyages were to England; included in the fourth voyage were eleven shuttle crossings to the beaches of Normandy beginning on D-Day plus 4. Voyage 5 was to Peru and Chile for vital ores needed in the war

*Mrs. Ida Lee Starling, whose husband was head of the White House Secret Service, launches the SS* Jeremiah O'Brien *on June 19, 1943. San Francisco Maritime National Historical Park.*

*Sliding down the ways, the SS* Jeremiah O'Brien *makes contact with the ocean for the first time.* National Liberty Ship Memorial.

effort. In Voyage 6 she loaded ammunition and bombs in Texas which she delivered to the Philippines and New Guinea. Her final voyage took her to Australia, India, China, the Philippines and again to Australia. By then, the war had ended and she brought twelve war brides and their children to San Francisco. She was then laid up in the Suisun Bay Reserve Fleet (mothball fleet) at Benicia, California on March 26, 1946.

There she languished until a group of volunteers, made up of active and retired merchant mariners, reconditioned her engine and sailed her out of the mothball fleet on October 6, 1979. Following a shipyard overhaul she was then taken to San Francisco's Fort Mason and began receiving visitors.

In 1994, crewed entirely by volunteers, she made an epic six-month voyage from San Francisco to England to take part in

*The 50th Anniversary of the landings in Normandy included* L'Armada de la Liberté *in Rouen, France (in the background). Note the crowds of people on the esplanade alongside the ships and the S.S.* Jeremiah O'Brien *in the center.* Author's collection.

the 50th Anniversary of the landings at Normandy. Of the entire armada of some 5,000 ships involved in the memorable D-Day landings, she was the only one to return.*

In recent years, the S.S. *Jeremiah O'Brien* has been berthed at pier 45 in San Francisco. She is still manned and operated by volunteers. The volunteers are mostly former merchant seamen, although we have several sons and daughters of seamen, a few grandsons and granddaughters, and several others who are

---

\* For the complete history of the S.S. Jeremaih O'Brien, see *SS Jeremiah O'Brien, The History of a Liberty Ship From the Battle of the Atlantic to the 21st Century*, by Capt. Walter W. Jaffee. For the history of all the Liberty Ships, see *The Liberty Ships From A(A.B. Hammond) to Z(Zona Gale)*, by Capt. Walter W. Jaffee. Both are available at www.glencannon. com or from the *Jeremiah O'Brien*'s ship's store.

enthusiastic about steam engines, old ships, World War II radio equipment, or who simply enjoy the act of volunteerism. Our enthusiasm is unbridled. We fondly remember the ships we were on and, to some extent, relive those experiences on the *Jeremiah O'Brien.*

With an operating budget of more than $1,000,000 a year, we scramble for every dollar we can get. Our revenue comes from day cruises; Fleet Week in October with the Blue Angels flying over San Francisco Bay is our biggest money maker. We offer other day cruises, but they carry fewer passengers and make fewer dollars. We also make a healthy revenue from visitors (tourists and maritime aficionados) who wander down the dock and pay to come aboard and tour the ship. Other revenue comes from the overnight program, in which girl scouts, boy scouts, cub scouts and sea scouts pay to spend a chaperoned night on board. Other revenue comes from donations, special dinners cooked on board in exchange for donations, revenue from the ship's store, silent auctions during cruises, raffles during cruises, and renting out the ship, or areas of the ship, for special occasions.

This may seem like a lot of sources of revenue, but against that there are the costs of drydocking (more than $500,000) every four years, monthly fees for electricity, berthing, garbage removal, a shoreside office, telephones, postage, printing — in other words all the normal costs of operating a business in a major metropolitan area, in addition to the required costs to keep the vessel "in class" and in presentable condition.

In short, we welcomed the idea of having the 2013 America's Cup match in San Francisco. We were on the fifty-yard line, front row, center. We knew how to handle people. We should be able to offer spectators a front row seat, *par excellence.* And, we could certainly use the money this historic event was scheduled to generate.

Would that it were that simple …

# 37

# IF ANYTHING CAN
# GO WRONG ...

In early 2011, Larry Ellison explained to San Francisco's then-Mayor Gavin Newsom and a crowd of VIPs his vision for the San Francisco America's Cup regatta in 2013. At the time he stood on the red-carpeted steps of city hall. Next to him was the newly acquired America's Cup itself. He planned to make the next regatta unlike any in the history of yacht racing.

"We're holding this cup in the San Francisco Bay, the most spectacular natural amphitheater for sailing that God created on this Earth," he said.

"And hundreds of thousands of people will be able to watch these races whether they're from Crissy Field, office buildings in downtown San Francisco, over in Sausalito or anyplace on the shoreline."

What he said next, however, would eventually come back to bite him: "I believe we'll have more than fourteen teams, sixteen teams here representing more than a dozen countries throughout the world."

His projection was realistic, given the number of teams that had challenged for the event by then, with more projected to come. Perhaps there was a touch of enthusiasm and salesmanship in what he said. But the press and the public (fed by the press), latched on to the last part of the above sentence, ignoring "I believe." "Fourteen teams" was taken as a promise, a guarantee, rather than a simple straightforward estimate of what Ellison believed would happen.

The San Francisco Bay Area was ideal for the organizer's plans. It offered windy conditions, racing in sight of shore, a natural ampitheater from which to view the races, and a major city that would provide hospitality and entertainment for fans from around the world.

In the beginning it seemed a simple matter. The GGYC would provide the trophy, hold two preliminary ACWS regattas in 2012, and finish the match in 2013 with the Louis Vuitton Cup and the America's Cup races. San Francisco would get a world famous sporting event, draw tens of thousands of visitors each day, and, according to one study benefit to the extent of $1.4 billion for the region, creating 8,000 jobs in the process.

San Francisco agreed in principle with the GGYC on the form of the agreement during the summer of 2010. The city then held hearings throughout the fall concerning the use of the waterfront south of the Oakland Bay Bridge at Piers 30-32 for an America's Cup Village. This was called the southern option. In additional hearings the proposal was changed with the San Francisco Board of Supervisors moving the Village to Piers 27-29. This was termed the northern option. After still more hearings, the Board of Supervisors unanimously approved the northern option in mid-December, subject to further negotiations.

On December 31 San Francisco and the GGYC finally came to terms and San Francisco was announced as the host of

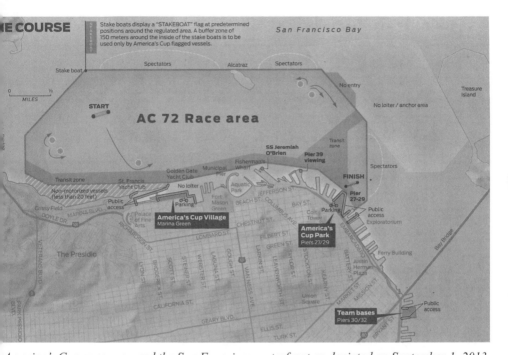

*America's Cup race area and the San Francisco waterfront as depicted on September 1, 2013.*
*the location of the S.S.* Jeremiah O'Brien, *just to the right of center.* San Francisco Chronicle.

the 2013 America's Cup. Piers 27-29 would host the public for the America's Cup. Marina Green and other locations along the northern waterfront would be prime viewing areas. Piers 30-32 would house the team facilities.

This was followed by a 2,500-page Environmental Impact Report which took six months to develop. There were more hearings, comments and revisions to the report, adoption of the report by the city, a lawsuit by local community groups disputing the adoption of the report, potential delays in construction and a settlement of $225,000 with the community groups in exchange for their withdrawal of the lawsuit.

Meanwhile a complicated arrangement whereby Larry Ellison would pay to refurbish Piers 27-29 and 30-32, let them be used for the event, then have them leased back to him as compensation for the cost of repairs, fell apart. In the end the only things improved were Piers 27-29, where the city built a cruise ship terminal, allowed the America's Cup to use it as America's Cup Park, and took it back once the races were over. Oracle Team USA had to use Pier 80, in the south bay and not accessible to the public, as their base. Team Artemis rented a seaplane hanger across the bay in Alameda. Emirates Team New Zealand and Luna Rosa were allowed the portions of Piers 30-32 that were considered safe (much of that area was, and is, not), for their bases.

In the end, time and lack of money prevented anything more extravagant.

At a press conference in February 2012 held at Oracle Team USA's Pier 80 base, the question of the small number of challengers was raised. At that time only Sweden's Artemis Racing, Emirates Team New Zealand, and their training partner, Luna Rossa, had paid the $200,000 entry fee that was due by June 1. The fizzling international economic climate loomed heavily in the background.

Russell Coutts, CEO, Oracle Team USA:

> The situation in Europe obviously affects things. There are four teams out there building two AC72s, three other syndicates that are going to be two boat programs. For the one boat programs, you don't actually have to announce that you are building a boat until June 1. There is at least one other single-boat [challenger] that will be or might have already started building a boat. So I think we will see other teams before the so-called Big Four teams. But even eight of these AC72s out on San Francisco Bay? I think that will be pretty cool to see.

Despite Coutts' enthusiasm and hopes, the Big Four would be the only boats in the Louis Vuitton and America's Cup finals.

Emirates Team New Zealand launched their first AC72 in July 2012. Oracle Team USA followed with their first in late August. By mid-October Luna Rossa was making ready to launch their first at Auckland. Artemis Racing's boat was being assembled and was almost ready to be put in the water.

Recovering from breaking a daggerboard on the first day of sailing in August, Oracle Team USA made a temporary repair using a daggerboard from their trimaran which had won the Cup in 2010. By mid-September the yacht was back in the water. On October 1, their fourth day of practice, they started getting the boat up, flying on her foils at times. On October 16 they were training in an increasing 20-knot wind, with gusts over 30 knots, and a strong ebb tide. After a fast upwind run, the helm was put over and the yacht turned to begin the downwind work. Bearing away (turning from upwind to downwind) on a multihull changes

*On October 16 the Oracle team USA AC72 accidentally dug her bows in on a turn and pitchpoled. Note the crew members hanging on. www.telegraph. co.uk*

the balance of forces on the boat and can be antsy, at best. As they changed course, they were caught by more wind than expected, in the steepest seas of the day, and made the turn more slowly than they should have. The maneuver placed a great deal of force on the bows, pushing them under. Unable to reduce the force, the boat pitchpoled, capsizing forward over her partially submerged bows.

At first she floated on her mast and the fore part of both hulls. She was then turned on her side with her mast still in the water. The crew was accounted for and there were no major injuries. Unfortunately the main spar of the wing then snapped, breaking the wing in two. The platform of the hulls and crossbeams was damaged, the development schedule was in shambles and the team was somewhat stunned to see their new boat become wreckage in such short order. By the time support boats arrived to tow the remains of the boat to her home base, she had drifted through the Golden Gate and out into the Pacific Ocean. It was a long, slow journey home.

Safety issues with the AC72s had been a topic when the new design was first revealed. Theoretically the boats were exciting, but match racing them around an inshore course was risking uncharted territory. Most informed observers agreed that one of these boats capsizing was not "if" but "when." Rumors began circulating about the wisdom and feasibility of racing such extreme boats.

Artemis Racing's first generation AC72, named *Artemis Red*, was the only boat of the AC72s built not to foil.* She was also the last of the first generation boats in the water. Arriving in San Francisco in August 2012, her platform had been assembled in Valencia, Spain and shipped on the deck of a freighter. On October 19, the morning of the yacht's naming ceremony, her platform was damaged during a towing test on the bay. It was another twenty-six days before she was launched. She sailed for the first time on November 14.

---

\* Foiling comes from the curved, horizontal portion of the daggerboards and horizontal wing-like plates mounted low on the rudders. As the boat increases speed they lift the hull up and out of the water causing it to foil.

Although Artemis Racing had an agreement with Oracle Team USA to sail practice sessions together, with the idea of sharing information within the limits of the Protocol, they spent twenty-three days sailing alone due to Oracle Team USA's boat being repaired from the pitchpoling incident. On February 13, 2013 Artemis Racing (with their non-foiling boat) and Oracle Team USA (with their foiling boat) sailed together for the first time. The foiling boat beat the non-foiling boat at every turn, clocking greater speed both upwind and downwind. It was obvious, the non-foiler was non-competitive.

Artemis took their red boat out of the water and began a rapid learning curve on the art of foiling. A pair of foils was attached to an AC45 for their sailing team to develop their skills in hydrofoiling a multihull. At the same time their red boat received several modifications, but without foils. Their second generation AC72, *Artemis Blue*, still under construction, was also modified — with the addition of foils. This modification would take some time and push her launch date back, but there was no choice. She would not be competitive otherwise.

Artemis' red boat was returned to the water on March 22, without foils, as the team continued working on tactics, tuning, boat handling, and teamwork. They also tested soft sail shapes, hard wing trim and fine-tuned their non-foiling skills, anticipating the Louis Vuitton Cup Races in July.

On May 9, Artemis Racing was sailing the red boat in winds in the mid-twenty knot range with gusts into the 30s. Nathan Outteridge was at the helm under the tutelage of multihull veteran Loïck Peyron. Suddenly over the radios of the other boats on the bay came the word that the Artemis boat had capsized. Images and reports came in revealing a port hull snapped in two pieces near the stern, the wingmast broken and limp in the water. Support boats from other teams rushed to the scene, pulling crewmembers from the water. After a few minutes a rescue boat was seen carrying a crewmember to shore, meeting an ambulance on the breakwater near the Golden Gate Yacht Club. Emergency responders were

*The Swedish* Artemis Red *broke up while training on May 9. One crew member was lost.* www.toledoblade.com.

trying to save someone. Soon word was received that it was too late. Nothing more could be done.

The deceased crewmember was Andrew "Bart" Simpson, a 36-year-old husband and father of two young boys. He was well-liked in the America's Cup community and had won Olympic Gold and Silver medals in 2008 and 2012 respectively.

Had the boat broken up while sailing or was the break up caused by capsizing? It happened so quickly that no one knew. The reaction outside the America's Cup community was a whirlpool of conjecture, hindsight and second guessing. Lack of facts was no barrier to fingers pointing in all directions. Monohull sailors were quoted on television saying multihulls were too dangerous. Multihull sailors blamed it on the wingsail. Some on the Internet blamed it on hydrofoils, despite the fact that *Artemis Red* was the only boat not equipped with them. Non-sailors blamed the organizers for sailing boats that were too fast, while others blamed

*Winner of medals in two Olympics, Andrew "Bart" Simpson, was lost when the Swedish boat broke up.* abcnews.go.com

them for sailing at all. Every piece of negative news related to the America's Cup was aired and thrown into stories questioning the event's existence.

On May 14, 2013, America's Cup organizers announced what was being done to improve safety and continue the America's Cup regatta. A review panel would be formed consisting of six international yachting experts. Their purpose would be to evaluate and determine what changes should be made to existing policies and procedures to make the Louis Vuitton Cup and America's Cup races safer for all concerned. On May 22 the review panel issued a list of thirty-seven AC72 safety recommendations.

There would be third-party structural reviews of all AC72 platforms and wings, performed confidentially. The maximum speed allowed for racing would be reduced to 20 knots during the Round Robin, 21 knots in the Louis Vuitton Cup Semi-Finals and 23 knots in the America's Cup Match (down from 33 knots).

The number of Round Robin races per boat would be reduced from seven to five to allow more time to maintain and repair boats in proportion to racing them.

If a yacht capsized during racing, it would be disqualified to allow immediate rescue without hesitation on the part of chase boats.

Crew safety was improved, particularly when it came to locator technology. Each crew member was given a personal strobe device to make him visible to rescuers. Each was also given a "keychain" he could click to send a signal that he was safe, thus creating an electronic head count. Requirements were upgraded for hands-free underwater breathing apparatus and high-visibility markings on crew helmets and uniforms.

Additional recommendations included requiring additional divers and swimmers on hand during training or racing and including paramedics and AED defibrillator devices on rescue boats.

The film covering the lower portion of the wingsail was to be made clear so crewmembers could be seen in places where they were likely to fall.

Race Management decided to replace the boats marking the start, finish and turns with inflatable buoys.

There would no longer be a penalty for not sailing a scheduled race. This was double-edged; on one side a crew would not feel pushed to sail when they thought conditions weren't safe, on the other, if a boat doesn't sail in a race it has no chance of getting points in that race, toward the final outcome.

Generally, the teams agreed with and were appreciative of the changes — at first. As time passed there developed objections over two issues (all changes required unanimous approval). The first involved changes to the rudder. The second was an increase in sailing weights to allow for structural improvements.

The rudders were to be made deeper with larger wings on them to permit increased stability. Emirates Team New Zealand objected on the basis that they had built their boat according to the original rules, making it stable at the sacrifice of performance. Changing the existing rudder would give them less of an edge in the competition, which, at this time, as was apparent in training runs, they had.

Artemis, still working hard to finish their second generation AC72, *Artemis Blue*, made structural reinforcements which put them overweight by Class rule. They needed a 100 kg. variance to compete. As official Challenger Of Record they also had veto power over any changes.

Arguments between the Challengers, the Defender, America's Cup Race Management (ACRM) ensued. Protests were filed. The matter went to a jury. In the end the method of ACRM's changes was rejected, Artemis was granted a waiver to use their existing runners and maintain their modified weight. Racing could proceed.

On July 26, 2013 as ACRM members prepared the AC45 yachts for the Red Bull Youth America's Cup Regatta they discovered an unusually heavy kingpost on the boat assigned to Team BAR (Ben Ainslie Racing). It was five pounds heavier than specified. Further investigation revealed the inside of the kingpost contained a mixture of resin and lead tailings. AC45 Class rules prohibited adding weights to kingposts.

Oracle Team USA (OTUSA) was notified because they owned the boat. Oracle launched an internal investigation and, on August 4, reported the issue to the International Jury, which began their own investigation. It was soon discovered that the BAR boat was not the only one modified in that manner.

Ben Ainslie was forthcoming, stating that the BAR boat "... was loaned the AC45 for competition by OTUSA and the boat was prepared/maintained by OTUSA. As skipper of the boat, I had no knowledge whatsoever that the boat was being raced out of measurement."

A day later the Oracle Team USA voluntarily asked to be retired retroactively (losing all their points for that series) and admitted "that prior to racing in the regattas the yachts were modified without the permission of the Measurement Committee."

Russell Coutts explained: "After the discovery, we had our designers run the VPP to determine the impacts to the weight. I think the finding was the weight would induce something like a 1/100th of a degree angle change in the boat. The performance impact was hardly measurable. It induced a near insignificant improvement upwind and a similarly small detriment to downwind speed."

The jury began interviews and hearings to investigate the case. In the end the jury cleared the team's upper management, which included Russell Coutts, Jimmy Spithill and general manager Grant Simmer. However they found five members of OTUSA in breach of the rules. Of these three were dismissed outright, one was suspended for the first four races and one was given a warning.

The jury levied two penalties against Oracle Team USA for violating Article 60.1 of the Protocol, which has to do with protecting the reputation of the America's Cup. The first penalty was a two-point loss in the America's Cup match. In other words,

Oracle Team USA would have to win 11 races to retain the Cup, while the challenger needed only 9 to take the trophy home.

The second penalty was that OTUSA was fined $250,000, half to go to the Andrew Simpson Sailing Foundation and the other half to go to a 501(c)(3) charitable organization selected by the mayor of San Francisco to provide support to at-risk youth in the San Francisco Bay Area.

Russell Coutts was outraged: "We've got penalized two points in the match for something that a few of our sailors did on an AC45 more than a year ago without the knowledge or approval of management or the skippers. I think it's an outrageous decision."

Fair or not, the penalties were within the guidelines of the Protocol and administered by an independent body. The effect of the penalties, while distracting to the event and demoralizing to Oracle Team USA, was transitory, and overcome by teamwork and good sportsmanship — as we will discover in the next chapter.

On a much smaller scale, but equally as important to those involved, was the potential for the SS *Jeremiah O'Brien*. Her newsletter, *Steady As She Goes*, for the spring of 2011 set out our expectations:

> The 34th America's Cup brings the competition for the oldest trophy in international sport back to the United States for the first time in 18 years. The preliminary estimate of money flowing into the Bay Area because of the Cup races exceeds $1.5 billion.
>
> The S.S. *Jeremiah O'Brien* is only asking for its share.
>
> America's Cup is essentially controlled by two organizations: America's Cup Race Management (ACRM) has operational control over everything that has to do with the race itself, such as the course and what kind of boats. The second organization is America's Cup Event Authority, which has operational control over the marketing, media and hospitality surrounding the race. It is the latter organization that the J.O'B. wants to do business with ...

The *Jeremiah O'Brien* has already been approached by the Event Authority about possible rental of the ship because it presents a stable, floating platform with height. America's Cup holds a lot of fundraising promise for the J. O'B. This column will keep you informed.

## Linda Greig, volunteer docent:

We had heard the hoopla about the America's Cup coming to San Francisco. It would be the first time that viewers along the waterfront could be spectators to the race. In the past, I guess that to view the races you would have to get someone to give you a ride on their boat or pay to go aboard one of the fancy regatta boats to see the race up close.

Our volunteer crew has expertise and experience in courteously handling the public on our historic vessel. We are well-motivated, ever conscious of the cost of maintaining the ship, and aware of the constant need for income to support her. We eagerly looked forward to the financial benefits of the America's Cup match.

## Linda Greig, volunteer docent:

I was in my car, driving along the crest of one of the city's many hills when I saw a faraway mast, zipping through the skyline of the rooftops of Fisherman's Wharf! It was huge, even from a distance of about two miles! The mast was moving quickly across my field of vision and it was hard to concentrate on traffic because everyone else saw it and was as amazed as I was.

I later came to find out that these sailing vessels are nothing like anything that have sailed before. They don't actually touch the water when going full speed, they cut through the water on stilt-like struts called hydrofoils, eliminating the water's drag on the hull. They can go much faster than the wind!

Being on Pier 45 on the aft gun tub of the *Jeremiah O'Brien* gave the us some of the best views of the race course. The first preliminary races were interesting because the statisticians from the Oracle team came aboard to view their boat and their competitor's boats. They were mostly Aussies or Kiwis and they were watching intently with binoculars, commenting on different aspects of the boats' performances. They were overall a very jovial group.

The first disappointment came when it was discovered that our "stable, floating platform" would not be rented out by the America's Cup Event Authority. We had been handed off to a business known as the Golden Gate Arena (GGA). This caused confusion and some resentment among the crew. To explain what was happening, the acting chairman of our Board of Directors (National Liberty Ship Memorial or NLSM) sent the following out on June 12, 2013:

> The National Liberty Ship Board of Directors is considering a contract with Golden Gate Arena to market the ship for the next six months. The board has been talking to Golden Gate Arena for nearly a year. Originally, Golden Gate Arena proposed a much different and longer contract than the one under discussion now.
>
> Essentially, what it would provide is that Golden Gate Arena would be the ship's marketing partner, particularly for special event rentals and for the America's Cup racing series this summer and fall. The contract would be for six months only. If it works to the NLSM's satisfaction it might be renewed. But only if it works.
>
> Golden Gate Arena provides the marketing expertise for a high profile event like the America's Cup that we simply do not have. We do not have marketing professionals on this ship or in this crew. We do well when we offer limited events, like cruises, or the Fourth of July fireworks. The America's Cup is a major league event, which is why some of the arrangements, ticketing in particular are being handled by Giants Enterprises, the marketing arm of the baseball team. The America's Cup event is being conducted right off our stern; we have a once in a lifetime opportunity to make some revenue from this event. It is no secret that we need the revenue: Fleet Week, our big money cruise, is in serious jeopardy and we are facing a $1 million shipyard bill down the road. The ship can continue to run its own activities, as

we did with the memorial cruise, under the Golden Gate Arena contract. Despite what you might read in internet discussion groups, the NLSM can run its own operations. Nor is this a "sellout" to make money for someone else. The deal is a profit sharing arrangement: The GGA will generate revenue, invest money and split the revenue with the ship under a formula we are working out. It is also incorrect that this is some kind of a secret deal. Tom Huston appeared at a specially called crew meeting earlier this year, answered all questions raised and stayed afterward to talk to anybody who wanted to talk to him. Obviously, negotiations for an agreement are not held in public; they never are from labor negotiations to legal negotiations. The board welcomes input and there are provisions for crew comments in both writing, and if preferred in person. The board, as always is acting in good faith and for the best interests of the ship. Please remember, too, that every one of the members of the board of directors is a volunteer. Just like you.

Respectfully,
Jeffrey Dickow, (Acting Chairman – NLSM)

## Pat Burke, volunteer, deck dept.:

Tom Huston was the former COO/CCO of the America's Cup Event Authority. After he was let go by them in March 2012, he formed his own company, Golden Gate Arena. GGA had been trying to get a contract with the ship to be our marketing partner to arrange for and put on events using the ship as a platform, and in the process getting lots of free labor out of the crew. Net profits from these events were to be split (how?) between the ship and GGA.

## Hal Drummond, docent coordinator:

I am a little bit alarmed that we may enter into a formal agreement with GGA. So far they have not produced any real results or a definitive plan of action, only smoke and mirrors. Next month is the start of the America's Cup races and we are supposed to be a seating venue for the event. People working in the doghouse [dockside ticket booth] and those who have yachting club contacts are being asked about tickets etc. for the event. As of today we do not have any definitive information other than "go to the web."

The Golden Gate Arena began operating on our behalf even before having a signed contract. Internet referrals were set up and a few items appeared in the local newspapers.

At some point the contract was signed, allowing GGA receipts for tickets sales, with the ship receiving a percentage. We also loaned them either $25,000 or $35,000 (sources vary) in startup costs to get their operation set up on board. On racing days, they arranged for large screen television sets fore and aft, placed and manned cocktail bars (at high prices), brought seating on board for guests and tried to make the ship seem hospitable for the $110+ ticketholders.

Pat Dupes-Matsumoto, volunteer docent: "The event planner with which we worked purchased 'luxury lawn furniture' to lounge in while waiting and watching the races. They also had large screen televisions and fully staffed and stocked bars for the paying customers."

Wilma Fox, volunteer docent:

The outdoor TV's for viewing were a great idea. The TV's allowed viewing of the race where viewing was

*In all the months of almost daily newspaper articles and photos of America's Cup events, this is the only image of the S.S. Jeremiah O'Brien to appear. The original caption read: "Sailing fans aboard the Jeremiah O'Brien had a distinctive view of the final race of the challenger series." It appeared on August 26, 2013. San Francisco Chronicle.*

*Taken during the Louis Vuitton Cup races, race watchers are gathered on the after deck of the S.S.* Jeremiah O'Brien *with Alcatraz Island in the background.* Author photo.

obstructed. Still being able to be outdoors taking part in the event, being out on the water, even though tied up to the dock was great. It made those on board feel like they were apart of the race. The covered areas were great for foul weather.

## Dave Winter, volunteer, engine dept.:

... the vessel could have been better utilized. The entire event was not the financial windfall it could have been. The City of SF stumbled over their own greed, Larry Ellison escaped almost unscathed financially and the JOB and her volunteers were overtaxed by the demands made by the production outfit which we partnered with (indeed, they stiffed us on a loan we gave them to be able to put on a "viewing experience aboard").

One bone of contention was GGA did not want anyone on board during their events who had not bought one of their tickets.

While this might be understandable from GGA's point of view, it was anathema to the crew. It meant we were completely shut down on racing days to tourists and visitors, a major source of income to us, for the sake of a percentage of the receipts GGA generated for, as it turned out, poorly attended races. In addition the crew was expected to clean up GGA's mess after they left the ship each day.

At the time, Hal Drummond, docent coordinator said:

> We have some duties and responsibilities to the GGA
> to provide the ship and some services. This must be done
> in a workman like manner to meet the requirements of the
> contract.
>
> This is our chance to make a good first impression on
> the visitors which come aboard the JOB. They know noth-
> ing about the NSLM and GGA but they are on the ship as a
> visitor to see the races and explore the ship. These visitors
> are the future life blood of the JOB. If they leave and talk
> favorably about their time on the ship they may influence
> friends and others to visit the ship or possibly join the crew.
> The ship has money making opportunities, other than rental
> paid by GGA, such as the store. We cannot afford to pass up
> needed revenue. By setting aside our feelings about GGA we
> can advance the JOB which should be our first priority.

Dave Winter, volunteer, engine dept.:

> The events that were put on aboard were classy for the
> viewers, but, on balance, I think more than a little part of the
> problem was attracting a champagne crowd on a blue collar
> platform. Note that volunteer resistance aboard certainly
> contributed to the difficulty the producer had in setting up
> what he wanted to do to prepare the platform before the
> event took place.

Wilma Fox, volunteer docent:

> There was confusion between the visitors who just
> wanted to view the ship and those who paid to watch and
> take part the America's Cup festivities. What did their

tickets include when on Board? Vendor and volunteers had no communications [between them].

There was no understanding as to what was allowed and needed from the volunteers even when the Event Organizer was in charge of the ship. Not to mention the volunteers unwilling to help the Event Planner or work during the month due to personal reasons.

## Pat Dupes-Matsumoto:

The plan was that the ship would not be open to the public on the day of the races and crew was not to come to the ship unless they were working the event. The ship would only be open to the visitors who paid a premium to come aboard to see the race.

That meant that needed work on the ship wasn't getting done on race days, especially if it were noisy, dirty, or potentially dangerous. It also meant that the regular crew that would operate the doghouse and patrol the ship wouldn't be there, so it would be difficult, maybe impossible, to open the ship to tourists, if the race was cancelled. A major loss. It never made sense to me to close the ship to regular traffic on race days.

One thing GGA, and many other business-oriented people don't seem to understand is that volunteers are there because of their passion for what they are doing. They don't have to be there. They cannot be fired, they cannot have their wages docked (they don't have any), they cannot be forced or ordered to do things they don't want to do. Success depends on working *with* them rather than them working *for* someone else.

One highlight in all this was when the America's Cup trophy was brought on board for two hours of public viewing. While our paying visitors enjoyed the event (it was a non-racing day), GGA inexplicably insisted that anyone holding one of their tickets be allowed on board free.

Wilma Fox, volunteer docent: "The day the America's Cup Trophy came onboard was another great event we probably could have made more of an event of."

Once the races were over, GGA disappeared. Rumor has it that they left owing the ship somewhere between $25,000 and $35,000. Other rumors have them and/or Tom Huston declaring bankruptcy.

Wilma Fox, volunteer docent:

> We missed a great opportunity to make some money. Allowing a company to rent out our ship was not a necessity. We should have been able to plan our own events around the dates of the races. Maybe offering with clarification special event days and tickets that included all day viewing of the America's Cup leading into the race, food and drinks.
>
> Nothing was done by the Event Company that we could not have organized and arranged ourselves.

Pat Dupes-Matsumoto, volunteer docent:

> I think everybody was incredibly naive about the whole America's Cup. The city of San Francisco looked to this as a certain moneymaker that would bring large crowds and moneyed observers to the city and it just never paid off. We heard wonderful predictions about the money that would be made that would pay for civic improvements that would need to be done to host the event, but it all sounded so much like the experiences of other cities that had hosted the Olympics, only to find out that they never saw the pots of gold.

Bob Bliss, volunteer docent: "It was a good experience for the ship and crew and I would hope that we all learned something from it. I'm sure there will be other events in and on the bay in which we might participate so we shouldn't get discouraged by the promoters that we dealt with at the Cup."

# 38

# FASTER THAN THE WIND

reated by Larry Ellison, the run-up to the America's Cup
finals in 2013 was unlike anything ever seen. It involved
a new class of yacht, the AC45 and AC72 catamarans. It
was aimed at reducing the overall costs of competing. It would
bring live ocean sail racing up close to more people throughout
the world than ever before. It would encourage young people to
become interested in the sport. It would be shown on television
in a quantum leap of technology that would make it understandable, exciting and entertaining.

It began with the America's Cup World Series (ACWS).
These were the first events for the new AC45s and a great opening
series. Sailors and organizers were able to fine tune their skills
and techniques. For the first time in twenty years, championship
races were shown on national TV (NBC) in the United States.
More than 10,000 people a day paid to watch the racing from
offshore in Newport, Rhode Island. Overall the ACWS regattas

265

enabled organizers and crews to work out the rules of racing fast catamarans on tight courses, developed the best ways to apply LiveLine technology, and improved everyone's skills in engaging large numbers of people with online and broadcast technology. These regattas reset everybody's expectations, proving how fast the new America's Cup action would unfold, and what it would take to keep up with it.

For the ACWS the AC45 had evolved to the following specifications:

> Build: honeycombcore carbonfiber sandwich
> Length: 44.1 ft.
> Beam: 22.6 ft.
> Weight: 2,840–2,910 lb.
> Maximum draft : 8 ft. 10 in.
> Air draft : 71 ft. without extension, 84 ft. with extension
> Wing: 66 ft. (899 sq. ft. wing element with three slotted
>     flaps)
> Extension: 13 ft. high, 94 sq. ft. area
> Jib area: 520 sq. ft., manufactured by a sail loft of team's
>     choice
> Gennaker area: 1,350 sq. ft., manufactured by a sail loft
>     of team's choice
> Builders: Core Builders (NZ), Cookson Boats (NZ)
> Crew: 5 + 1 guest

The first regatta was held in Cascais, Portugal in August 2011. This was followed by Plymouth, England in September, and San Diego, California in November. The 2012 regattas were held at: Naples, Italy in April; Venice, Italy in May; Newport, Rhode Island in June-July; and, San Francisco, California in August and again in October. The last ACWS match was held in Naples, Italy in April of 2013.

The teams represented in the ACWS were: South Korea Yacht Club from South Korea, one boat; Artemis Racing from

*The America's Cup World Series in Naples in April 2012 for the first time gave spectators an up close view of America's Cup yacht racing. www.charterworld. com*

Sweden, two boats; Emirates Team New Zealand from New Zealand, one boat; Oracle Racing from the United States, two boats; China Team from China, one boat; Energy Team from France, one boat; Aleph Sailing Team from France, one boat; Real Club Náutico de Valencia from Spain, one boat; Circolo della Vela

*Team Oracle Racing and team Luna Rossa (Prada) in close competition at Naples. www.charterworld.com*

*The HS Racing (United States) AC45 on the edge of capsizing in Venice.* www. charterworld.com

Sicilia from Italy, two boats; and, Royal Cornwall Yacht Club from Australia, one boat.

The America's Cup World Series ran two competitions: one for 2011-2012 and one for 2012-2013. Oracle Racing won both competitions with the most points in each, but was later disqualified. This left Emirates Team New Zealand the winner of the first competition and Luna Rossa (Circolo della Vela Sicilia) winner of the second. The points did not carry over to subsequent races as those would deal with a different type of boat, the AC72.

With slight modifications, the AC72 had evolved to the following maximum specifications:

Length overall: 86 ft.
Waterline length: 72.2 ft.
Beam: 45.9 ft.
Weight: 13,000 lb.
Maximum draft: 14 ft.
Crew: 11

With only three challengers, Emirates Team New Zealand, Luna Rossa Challenge and Artemis Racing, the Louis Vuitton Cup match (to determine who would face Oracle in the America's Cup match) was to begin with five Round Robins, ten races per boat, fifteen races total. Because of Artemis' earlier difficulties and the amount of time needed to prepare their second boat, the Swedish team announced they would not be ready to race until the semi-final round. This left two teams able to sail.

Each Round Robin race was worth one point to the winning boat. While no team could be eliminated during the Round Robin series, whichever team had the most points at the end of the series had the right to choose how the teams advanced into the semi-final and final rounds and what the pairings in those rounds would be. The semi-final and final rounds would eliminate the loser of each match from competition.

Artemis would receive zero points for each race it missed and would be scored as DNS (Did-Not-Start). But for either of the other two boats to score points, they had to race the course from start to finish, whether or not another boat was involved. This resulted in two-thirds of the Round Robin races featuring a single boat running the course. It seemed silly, the viewing public didn't understand or enjoy it, but it was necessary according to the rules.

July 7, 2013 was to be the first race between two AC72s. Although scheduled, Luna Rossa did not race, in protest because a complaint it filed about safety regulations had not yet been ruled on by the America's Cup jury. Instead, only New Zealand's boat ran, completing the seven-leg course in forty-six minutes and earning one point.

On July 9 New Zealand was scheduled to race against Artemis, which was still working on its boat. New Zealand again completed the course, earning a second point.

Luna Rosa went out on July 11, Artemis stayed in port, and the first cycle of the Round Robin was done. The score was 2-1 in New Zealand's favor with none of the boats having actually raced against another.

The first race in the second cycle of the Round Robins on July 13, pitted Emirates Team New Zealand against the Italian's Luna Rossa. It was eagerly looked forward to; after three years of anticipation, the first competition between AC72s. ETNZ took an eight second lead across the start line, increased the lead to twenty-nine seconds at the downwind gate and built on that with each subsequent leg. ETNZ won by five minutes, twenty-three seconds. Because the Racing Rules for Sailing for the America's Cup specified that a race was terminated five minutes after the first boat crossed the finish line, Luna Rossa was officially declared DNF (Did-Not-Finish).

The Kiwis gained another point the following day when Artemis again did not appear and they sailed the course alone.

Linda Greig, volunteer, S.S. *Jeremiah O'Brien*: "Once the races actually got underway in July, it was clear that the Kiwis boat was the fastest of all. It made the Italian boat, *Luna Rossa*

*The New Zealand team making the turn well ahead of Luna Rossa increased her lead and was easily ahead at the Finish Line in the first race of the second cycle.* www.elblogdethornado.blogspot.com

*Emirates Team New Zealand whistling along at more than 40 knots, which they seemed to do frequently.* www.bbc.co.uk

look like it was carrying a cargo of bricks."

Two days later Luna Rossa gained another point in the same manner.

At the completion of the Round Robins, Emirates Team New Zealand was ahead with nine points (4 race wins, 5 forfeit wins) to Luna Rossa Challenge's four points (4 forfeit wins) and Artemis Racing's zero points.

The Round Robins were an opportunity for the competing teams to hone their skills and improve their tactics, giving a glimpse of what was to come. The most exciting occurrence in this event was the Kiwi boat achieving 44.1 knots (more than 50 miles an hour) in 15 to 17 knot winds. This occurred in Round Robin 3 on July 18.

Once ETNZ's lead in the Round Robins was assured they opted out of the remainder of the series to add modifications to their boat. As winner of the Round Robins, they also decided to skip the semi-finals. This was probably a bit of gamesmanship on their part, keeping the other teams off-balance, wondering what they were doing to their boat.

The Louis Vuitton Cup semi-finals began on August 6 with an elimination round between Luna Rossa and Artemis Racing, running their newly foiled and recently placed in the water *Artemis Blue*. The first to win four races would go to the Louis Vuitton Cup final. In the first race, Artemis lead Luna Rossa across the Start Line, but the Italian boat quickly took the lead with better downwind speed and won by two minutes. The second race was similar to the first, with the Swedish boat losing time on the gybes while the Italians demonstrated the value of having more experience in foiling on turns. Luna Rossa won in two minutes, five seconds. In Race 3 Luna Rossa started with a small lead, which slowly increased to give them a third win. Race four clinched it for the Italians. Artemis had overcome a great deal of bad fortune and tragedy with wonderful sporting effort. Sadly, their America's Cup effort, which cost in excess of $100 million brought them four losses. They were no longer in the competition.

Final races for the Louis Vuitton Cup began on August 17 and were a best of thirteen series, meaning to win the cup a team had to win seven races. Although disqualified in race two with a hydraulic failure, Emirates Team New Zealand took races 1 and 3 through 8 to win and place herself as the challenger to the America's Cup.

The Red Bull Youth America's Cup, aimed at developing interested young sailors in America's Cup racing, was held after the Louis Vuitton Cup and before the America's Cup match.

Eight races were held with two each day on Sunday, September 1; Monday, September 2; Tuesday, September 3 and Wednesday, September 4. The field included ten international teams. The boats were AC45 catamarans powered by wing sails, the same boats used by the America's Cup teams in the AC World Series from 2011-2013. Each team was composed of six sailors, aged 19-24, who represented their country through a nationality rule.

*Luna Rossa shows the form that earned the Italian team four straight wins and entry to the Louis Vuitton Cup finals.* www.juanpanews.com

Races would be fleet races, twenty-five minutes long with 10 points awarded for first place, nine for second and so on. After the first day of racing the standings were: 1. New Zealand Sailing Team (New Zealand), 16 points; 2. Next World Energy (France), 15; 3. (tie) Full Metal Jacket Racing (New Zealand), Swedish Youth Challenge (Sweden) and American Youth Sailing Force (U.S.) 14; 6. ROFF/Cascais Sailing Team (Portugal), 13; 7 (tie) Team Tilt (Switzerland) and All In Racing (Germany), 9; USA 45 Racing (U.S.), 4; Objective Australia (Australia), 2.

*Emirates Team New Zealand foiling quickly past the San Francisco waterfront during the Louis Vuitton Cup finals.* Lee Ditlefsen.

*The first day of the Red Bull Youth America's Cup, at this point has Germany, Sweden, New Zealand and the U.S.A. racing together.* Lee Ditlefsen.

After the sixth race the standings were: 1. NZL Sailing Team; 2. (tie) Full Metal Jacket Racing and Youth America Sailing Force; 4. Swedish Youth Challenge; 5. ROFF/Cascais Sailing Team; 6. Team Tilt; 7. Next World Energy; 8. Objective Australia; 9. All In Racing; 10. USA 45 Racing.

In the end the New Zealand Sailing team placed first, that country's Metal Jacket Racing placed second, and ROFF/Cascais was third. American Youth Sailing Force finished fifth overall.

While spectators found the fleet racing of the Red Bull Youth America's Cup a refreshing and entertaining break from earlier events, they were eager for the main event — the America's Cup.

The course for the Cup was especially designed to take advantage of San Francisco Bay and bring racing within easy viewing of the shore for the first time. The starting area was the farthest point from the shore, close to the Golden Gate Bridge. The boats were allowed to enter the starting box two minutes before the gun. The boat entering on port tack was allowed to enter ten seconds before that on the starboard tack to reduce the danger of having two boats travelling at up to 40 knots heading towards each other into the starting area.

After the race gun signaled the start, the first leg was a short reach of around 0.5 nautical miles towards the shore. The second leg was about 2.5 nautical miles downwind. At the bottom of the course, the leeward gate had two marks. Rounding either mark

*Here, again on the first day, France leads both Portugal and the U.S.A. along the San Francisco waterfront.. Lee Ditlefsen.*

completed the leg. The third leg stretched more or less 3 nautical miles from the leeward gate to the windward gate. This upwind leg was the longest timewise, even though the AC72s were able to sail upwind at close to twice the speed of the wind against them. The windward gate also had two marks, with the skippers able to choose either to complete it. On the fourth and final downwind leg, the boats aimed for the leeward mark closer to shore. Rounding

*Ten catamarans manned by the youth from nations around the world line up on September 3 for the start of race 6 of the Red Bull Youth America's Cup.* San Francisco Chronicle.

this put them on a sprint to the finish. The fifth leg was around 1 nautical mile in length. The Finish Line was close in front of America's Cup Park, at Piers 27/29.

The length of the course varied, but was about 10 nautical miles (and generally took about twenty-five minutes). The course was marked by a boundary. Going outside of the boundary drew a penalty which was indicated by blue lights on board the boat that did so. Green lights on board flashed whenever a boat was within three boatlengths of a boundary, or a mark. Whichever boat entered the three boatlength circle around a mark would generally have mark rights and be allowed to round without worrying about the other boat. The exception was when there was an overlap between the two boats. If an overlap existed, room had to be made to ensure both boats rounded the mark safely. The maximum time for a race was forty minutes after which the race was stopped. If a penalty was awarded against a boat, a moving penalty line was calculated and placed two boat lengths behind them, advancing on a direct heading to the mark or the wind (depending on which leg they were on). The penalized boat had to slow their Velocity Made Good such that their boat fell behind the penalty line. This was calculated in real time by computers, and indicated to the teams on the water via the lights and radio communication.

Alcatraz Island was a unique part of the racecourse. For the first week of the event, San Francisco Bay experienced flood tides. As water flowed into the bay, there was a cone close to the Island where the incoming tide was noticeably less than along the rest of the racecourse. On the upwind leg, when boats had to sail against the flood tide, tactical use of this cone was crucial.

As mentioned in the previous chapter, an international jury found Oracle Team USA guilty of cheating during the America's Cup World Series warmup event in 2012. Penalties imposed included a one point penalty for each of the first two races of the Match in which they would otherwise score a point. This meant that Oracle had to win 11 races to retain the trophy, while New Zealand only needed to win 9 races to lift the cup.

The first day of the America's Cup match was September 7, 2013. There were two races. In the first, Team New Zealand skippered by Dean Barker, led at the first mark, and held it until the finish line, winning by thirty-six seconds. In the second race Team New Zealand led the entire race, and completed the victory by fifty-two seconds to lead 0–2.

On the following day, Race three at first looked good for Oracle, as Team New Zealand drew a penalty. Oracle held the lead for the first downwind leg, and were eighteen seconds to the good heading into the upwind third leg. But the New Zealand boat tacked within three boat lengths of the boundary forcing Oracle to tack away due to boundary rights. The lead at the top mark was held by the Kiwis all the way to the finish, crossing twenty-eight seconds ahead of the Americans to go up 0–3.

Race four again started well for Oracle, leading around the reach mark by six seconds. Spithill was able to hold off Team New Zealand to cross the finish line first by eight seconds. Due to the penalty imposed by the International Jury, Oracle was left at -1 and New Zealand at +3 points in the standings.

*Emirates Team New Zealand leads Team Oracle around the course, a situation seen far too often in the early races.* www.warwickdailynews.com.au

The third racing day was September 10. Oracle's defeat in race five by one minute, five seconds was so emphatic that the Americans played their one and only Postponement Card to call off the scheduled second race of the day. The score at the end of the day was -1 to 4, with Team New Zealand ahead.

By September 12, the fourth racing day, Oracle had changed their tactician, John Kostecki, for Sir Ben Ainslie, the skipper of Oracle's backup boat. Race six followed a familiar pattern, with Oracle ahead at the start and holding that lead to the bottom of the downwind leg. After rounding the mark twelve seconds behind, Team New Zealand once again took over sailing into the wind. The Kiwis gained fifty-five seconds during the third leg, and had a forty-seven second lead at the finish.

In race seven Team New Zealand led from start to finish. They ended the day with a record of -1 to 6, two-thirds of the way to lifting the America's Cup.

Two days later race eight brought Team New Zealand to the brink of disaster. Their hydraulic power failed at a crucial moment and the boat's starboard hull rose out of the water, coming within a degree of capsizing. In addition, the Kiwi boat was penalized for failing to give way to Oracle who was on starboard tack at the time. Oracle won by fifty-two seconds. Oracle's victory completed the penalty imposed by the International Jury, bringing them from -1 to 0, and allowing them to accrue points for any subsequent victories.

Team New Zealand was ahead during the third leg of the day's second race, but the race was abandoned by the Race Committee due to the wind exceeding the 22.6-knot allowable maximum (minus 0.4 knots for the tide).

Racing day 6 on September 15 began with race nine which showed Oracle Team USA at their best. Spithill won the start, and extended the lead at every mark including for the first time, a notable gain against the Kiwi boat on the upwind leg. Recording consecutive victories for the first time allowed Oracle to finally get a point, bringing the score to 1–6.

*In race eight, New Zealand's boat came within one degree of capsizing due to a hydraulic failure.* tvnz.co.nz

Team New Zealand won race ten by sixteen seconds, in what was widely reported as one of the most exciting America's Cup races of all time. Barker appeared to have been left behind by Spithill at the Starting Line, but just managed to hold an overlap as the AC72s entered the circle at the reach mark. Team New Zealand took a three second lead, and increased it to eleven at the second mark. Oracle again showed their new competitiveness during the upwind beat, and the lead changed three times. As the boats approached the top mark on split tacks, Barker slowed the boat, then aimed down to pass under Oracle at speed. The top mark split was only one second as Oracle rounded in front of the shore, and the Kiwi boat rounded the other mark. With the race still too close to call during the downwind leg, Spithill made the call to dip behind Team New Zealand rather than jibe. The gap almost instantly became 330 feet (100 meters). Barker held this lead to the finish to take the series to 1–7. In the post race press conference Barker said "If you didn't enjoy today's racing you should probably watch another sport."

On September 17 high winds postponed racing.

Linda Greig, volunteer, S.S. *Jeremiah O'Brien*:

The Kiwi boat performed the best by far, and it had accumulated an overwhelming lead. Out of nine races, they had won eight and they only needed one more! Then the next day, the weather conditions completely changed. Up to this point, the wind had been so brisk that there were many days the race had actually been cancelled due to excessive wind speed. But on the last day that the Kiwis needed to win to claim their victory — the wind died down to almost nothing. And yet the Kiwis still won that day. But then they were disqualified because they exceeded the maximum race time for the course!

At this point, I think that Larry Ellison, owner of the Oracle boat, realized that he better pull a rabbit out of his hat pretty quick — and somehow he did! He sidelined his boat and team and they made some adjustments. And then amazingly, they started winning race after race! They won nine straight races and made a stunning come-from-behind victory!

September 18, the eighth day of racing, found Team New Zealand leading all the way to win race eleven by fifteen seconds taking the score to 1–8. This was to prove to be the last win of the regatta for Emirates Team New Zealand.

The second race of the day suffered a fifteen minute wind delay postponement, as the boats hit the Starting Line. Then the wind and strong outgoing tide combined to postpone racing for the day.

Racing day 9, September 19, saw Spithill able to force New Zealand to keep clear. From that lead off the start line, Oracle led the entire way to win race twelve by thirty-one seconds on the line. Oracle gained their second point to take the score to 2–8.

The start time for the second race of the day was pushed back several times due to the wind exceeding the allowed limit and racing was finally postponed, allowing Oracle to stay alive for another day.

On September 20, racing day 10, the winds were the lightest seen in the 34th America's Cup. Oracle had the better start in the 8-knot winds, and luffed Team New Zealand at the reach mark. The first downward leg was very different from the rest of the racing, as neither boat was able to get up on its foils. The *Aotearoa* (the New Zealand boat) appeared to be the stronger vessel in the light breeze, and rounded the leeward gate one minute, forty-two seconds ahead of the Americans. The Kiwi boat extended their lead during the third leg and concern turned to whether they would be able to cross the finish line within the forty minute race limit. Unfortunately, time expired forcing the abandonment of the race.

The resail of race thirteen began at 2:33 P.M. in 12 knots of wind. Team New Zealand led over the line, and took a three second lead around the reach mark. The pivotal moment of the race came towards the end of the second leg. Team New Zealand was slightly ahead and tried to cross in front of Oracle who had the starboard tack advantage. Spithill had to evade the Kiwi boat, and gained a penalty for the infraction. With the boats still close heading into the leeward gate, Barker fluffed his lines, and the *Aotearoa* ended up being forced to jibe twice in quick succession. Oracle sped away to begin the third leg leaving the Kiwis almost dead in the water. Oracle confirmed their third point by one minute, twenty-four seconds at the finish. The New Zealanders' largest defeat of the Cup to date brought the score to 3–8.

On race day 11, September 21, the race committee pushed the start back several times hoping that the wind would turn enough to allow racing. This did not happen and weather again forced postponement of the day's racing.

September 22 was the twelfth day of racing. Race fourteen was another win by Oracle. They were twenty-three seconds ahead at the finish to bring the score to 4–8.

Team New Zealand led off the line for race fifteen, but the leeward position of the Oracle Team USA boat allowed them to round the reach mark first. A huge downwind leg from the American boat saw them round the leeward gate one minute ahead of the Kiwis. Oracle had their best day on the water yet, winning both races to bring the score to 5-8.

A day later the start of race sixteen was delayed for thirty minutes while the race committee waited for the wind to increase.

Emirates Team New Zealand took the leeward position at the start line but Oracle Team USA got onto its foils and sailed over on top of the Kiwis to lead by five seconds at the reach mark. At the second mark the New Zealand team was thirteen seconds behind Oracle and after a tacking duel upwind to the third mark Oracle was able to get the wind advantage for the downwind leg. Oracle sailed conservatively downwind gaining a twenty-one second lead for the fourth mark, which they extended to thirty-three seconds by finish line. The score was now 6–8 and it was their 5th straight win.

The earlier delay meant no second race for the day, as it would have exceeded the cutoff time of 2:40 P.M.

On September 24 race seventeen saw two penalties at the start against Emirates Team New Zealand: a right-of way violation, and a minor collision between the two boats. By the time the penalties were completed, Oracle was up by eighteen seconds at the reach mark. Oracle built on their lead and went on to win by twenty-seven seconds. The score: 7–8.

"We're not going to stop — we're going to keep going all the way to the end," said Spithill. "We really want this. You can sense it on board." Barker called this defeat "an absolute shocker" as he ended in "a really dead spot."

In race eighteen the Kiwis led at the start and up to the first mark. They set the speed record of the series, reaching 47.57 knots (55 mph) as they rounded the mark, to lead by five seconds. They kept the lead during the first downwind run, but Oracle got ahead at the first crossing on the upwind leg after the Kiwis made a poor tack. Team New Zealand had starboard tack advantage and the lead at the time, but did not properly cover Oracle. The American boat was up on the foils, and powered past the Kiwis. Oracle went on to lead by fifty-seven seconds at the windward gate and won by fifty-four seconds.

This tied the series 8–8 and forced a winner-take-all race. Spithill called this win "very impressive" and said, "It gives us a lot of confidence going into tomorrow," saying that Wednesday will be "the most exciting day in the history of our lives. We wouldn't want to be anywhere else."

The final day of the match, September 25, brought only the third winner-takes-all match in Cup history (previous such matches had occurred in 1920 and 1983).

Team New Zealand had port entry advantage, and were able to convert this into the leeward position at the start line and a lead around the reach mark. Oracle had a moment where both bows dipped into the water, slowing them to open some separation between the two boats. The first downwind leg saw both boats foiling at around 40 knots, at times, well within 330 ft. of each other. Team New Zealand took the lead into the upwind third leg, but were unable to hold it. Oracle once again showed their upwind foiling ability and were able to pass with ease. Team New Zealand and Barker refused to give up, but Oracle was ahead by forty-four seconds on the Finish Line to the cheers of the crowd. They had achieved an unbelievable come-from-behind victory, the most amazing in all sports, and won the America's Cup, keeping it again in America.

*The celebration begins!* latesttrendzs.blogspot.com

**AMERICA'S CUP**

# The comeback crew

## Team USA wins 'race of century' to retain cup

By Julia Prodis Sulek
*jsulek@mercurynews.com*

SAN FRANCISCO — Nobody believed Oracle Team USA skipper Jimmy Spithill when he called his crew the underdogs before the America's Cup finals began. And no one believed him when, down 8-1 against New Zealand, he said they were going to make the greatest comeback in sailing history.

But in a dramatic final showdown Wednesday that one commentator called the "race of the century," the team owned by software billionaire Larry Ellison proved everybody wrong. In an intense, come-from-behind victory, Oracle Team USA beat Emirates Team New Zealand by 44 seconds for the oldest trophy in international sports.

Triumphant, Spithill and his crew pumped their fists and

*See* **CUP**, *Page 6*

**ON A1**
Purdy: Team USA beats the odds for a historic victory.

JANE TYSKA/STAFF
Oracle Team USA crosses the finish line to win the America's Cup, completing a comeback from an 8-1 deficit. Afterward, team tactician Ben Ainslie drinks from the cup as he celebrates with crew

*The front page of the San Francisco Chronicle's sport section showed the Oracle boat approaching the Finish Line in the last race with New Zealand well behind.* San Francisco Chronicle.

# EPILOGUE

America's Cup yacht racing has always been a wealthy man's sport. That alone makes it worth studying. The wealthy are not like you and I. In addition to having a lot more money, they are able to live in their own world, from time to time brushing the fringes of ours, but mostly according to their own desires, values and sense of ethics. Viewing the history of the America's Cup from start to 2013 touches on the personalities of those wealthy and the impact they have had on our lives.

We have also seen the evolution of the America's Cup yacht from a quick, tall-masted boat equipped with owner's living quarters and amateur crews, to sleek, double-hulled vessels, stripped of all non-essentials, manned by paid professionals able to skim above the water's surface at speeds faster than the wind.

Through the years there have been changes in the racing rules, changes in nationality requirements, changes in the location of the event, changes in methods of testing boats and changes in the public's perception of what the America's Cup is all about. Our chance to experience the culmination of all this came to San Francisco in 2013.

I almost titled this book "Great Expectations," for everyone approached the event with just that. However, Charles Dickens used the title earlier and, when viewed from 1851 to 2013 the story was about more than that, plus the S.S. *Jeremiah O'Brien* was smack dab in the center of it all, hence *America's Cup From the Fifty-Yard Line*.

Larry Ellison came to San Francisco with the expectation of being treated as he was in the world's other major cities. He was sorely disappointed.

The city fathers of San Francisco expected Ellison to hand them millions of dollars so they could upgrade the city's languishing facilities. That never happened.

On the S.S. *Jeremiah O'Brien* we expected to get our piece of the financial pie. Likewise a non-occurance.

The spectators, whether viewing in person or on television, expected an exciting, action-filled series of races from start to finish; even if they didn't understand the America's Cup rules. It was there, if only they made the effort to learn what was going on.

Several things cast a cloud over America's Cup 2013 that forced everyone to deal with the disappointment of diminished and unfulfilled expectations. First there was the global economy. The entire world was in a deepening economic recession which began years earlier. Because of this yacht racing teams that planned to challenge for the America's Cup had to withdraw — the necessary funds were not there. The city of San Francisco had gone through a belt-tightening period that put them in a weak financial position. Second, the America's Cup regatta was hit with an unbelievable run of bad luck. Part of that was the global economy. Then came the loss of the Oracle boat that pitchpoled while practicing, followed by the capsizing and destruction of *Artemis Red*, the death of an Artemis Racing crew member in the same incident, Oracle teams's cheating incident, public apathy from watching races with one boat running the course, and poor attendance.

All of these incidents conspired against everyone's expectations. And rather than accept the situation for what it was, people, as humanity usually does in such situations, looked for someone to blame. Unwilling to settle the blame on concepts, they sought more tangible targets. Fingers were pointed at Larry Ellison, the city fathers of San Francisco, the media, the designers of the boats, boat crews, the weather and, sometimes, these were all lumped together and blamed as one.

Assigning blame usually accomplishes little except to make the person assigning blame feel resentfully self-righteous. Larry Ellison was blamed because he is a billionaire and people are envious but won't admit it. San Francisco city fathers were blamed because they are politicians. The media was blamed because they wrote and televised news, and the only news they write these days is negative; even if a story is upbeat, they focus on the negative to make it newsworthy. The S.S. *Jeremiah O'Brien* lacked leadership and was unable to capitalize on the event.

Sometimes fate simply dictates an outcome nobody wants. When that happens one must just get over it and move on.

In the end, America's Cup 2013 was a long, arduous competition with a storybook ending. Those who sailed the yachts probably enjoyed it the most. To them it was grand to be out on the water battling the elements and competing against one another. And maybe, just maybe, what all of this was really about was "the irrepressible elements of the wind and the sea and the fellowship of sport for its own sake."

# BIBLIOGRAPHY

Alvord, Douglas. *America's Cup, an Illustrated History.* Boston: Hanover Studios, 1977

Analyst, Budget and Legislative. "Policy Analysis Report." San Francisco: City and County of San Francisco, Board of Supervisors, February 10, 2014.

Bavier, Bob. *The America's Cup, An Insider's View — 1930 To the Present.* New York: Dodd, Mead & Company, 1980.

Beken, Frank & Keith. *The America's Cup, 1851 to the Present Day.* London: The Harvill Press, 1999.

Blackburn, Graham. *Overlook Dictionary of Nautical Terms.* Woodstock, N.Y.: The Overlook Press, 1981.

Bradford, Ernle. *The America's Cup.* London: Country Life Limited, 1964.

Brooks, Jerome E. *The $30,000,000 Cup, The Stormy History of the Defense of the America's Cup.* New York: Simon and Schuster, 1958.

Brouwer, Norman J. *International Register of Historic Ships.* Annapolis, Maryland: Naval Institute Press, 1985.

Bunker, John Gorley. *Liberty Ships, The Ugly Ducklings of World War II.* Annapolis: U.S. Naval Institute, 1972.

Carrick, Robert W. *Pictorial History of The America's Cup Races, The.* New York, New York: The Viking Press, 1964.

Carrick, Robert W. and Stanley Z. Rosenfeld, editors. *Defending the America's Cup.* New York: A;fred A. Knopf, 1969.

Coat, Tom. *A Cup of Controversy, The Intrigue Behind the Strangest America's Cup Ever.* n.p. 1988

Cohen, Susan. *Historic Preservation.* "World War II Ugly Duckling Comes Home." March-April 1980.

Cole, Mervyn C., compiler. *The America's Cup Cartoon Collection From Newspapers Around the World.* South Perth, Western Australia: Kara International PTY LTD, 1984.

Conner, Dennis. *Comeback, My Race For the America's Cup.* New York: St. Martin's Press, 1987.

Dear, Ian. *The America's Cup, An Informal History.* New York: Dodd, Mead & Company, 1980.

Dougherty, Kevin J. *Ships Of the Civil War, An Illustrated Guide to the Fighting Vessels of the Union and the Confederacy.* New York: Metro Books, 2013.

*The Encyclopaedia of the America's Cup In Stamps,* Perth, Western Australia: Philatelic International, 1987.

Fairchild, Tony. *The America's Cup Challenge: There Is No Second.* London: Nautical Books, 1983.

Fisher, Bob and, Kimball Livingston, Ivor Wilkins, Mark Chisnell, James Boyd. *Sailing on the Edge, America's Cup.* San Rafael, California: Insight Editions, 2013.

Gilbert, Cali. *It's Simply Sailing ... Our Voyage To the 2013 America's Cup.* Lexington, Kentucky: Cali Gilbert, 2012.

Guthrie, Julian. *The Billionaire and the Mechanic, How Larry Ellison and a Car Mechanic Teamed Up to Win Sailing's Greatest Race, the America's Cup.* New York: Grove Press, 2013

Haws, Duncan and Alex Hurst. *The Maritime History of the World - 2.* Brighton, Sussex: Teredo Books, Ltd. 1985.

Hughes, Terry and John Costello. *Battle of the Atlantic, The.* New York: The Dial Press/James Wade, 1977.

Huntington, Anna Seaton. *Making Waves, The Inside Story of Managing the First Women's Team to Compete for the America's Cup.* Irving, Texas: The Summit Publishing Group, 1996.

Johansen, Jon B. *America's Cup Trivia.* Brewer, Maine: Cay-Bel Publishing Co., 1986.

Kortum, Karl and Adm. Thomas J. Patterson. "How We Saved the *Jeremiah O'Brien.*" *Sea History.* Winter 1988-89.

Levingston, Steven E. *Historic Ships of San Francisco.* San Francisco: Chronicle Books, 1984.

Livingston, Kimball. *America's Cup San Francisco, The Official Guide.* San Rafael, California: Insight Editions, 2013.

Lindsay, Nigel. *The America's Cup.* London: Heath Cranton Limited, 1930.

McKeag, Malcolm. *Cudmore and the America's Cup, A Sailor's Perspective.* London: The Kingswood Press, 1987.

Riggs, Doug. *Keelhauled, Unsportsmanlike Conduct and the America's Cup.* London: Stanford Maritime Limited, 1986.

Rousmaniere, John. *A Picture History of the America's Cup.* Mystic, Connecticut: Mystic Seaport Museum Stores, 1989.

Rubin, Hal. "The Last of the 'Libertys'." *Oceans.* March 1979.

Sawyer, L.A. and W. H. Mitchell. *The Liberty Ships*, Second Edition. London: Lloyd's of London Press Ltd., 1985.

Sherman, Rev. Andrew M. *Life of Jeremiah O'Brien*. Morristown, N. J.: Jerseyman Office, 1902.

Shulman, Daniel. *Sons of Wichita, How the Koch Brothers Became America's Most Powerful and Private Dynasty*. New York: Grand Central Publishing, 2014.

Simpson, Richard V. *America's Cup, Trials & Triumphs*. Charleston, SC: The History Press, 2010.

Simpson, Richard V. *The Quest For the America's Cup, Sailing to Victory*. Charleston, SC: The History Press, 2012.

Stone, Herbert L. *The America's Cup Races*. New York: The Macmillan Company, 1930.

Stone, Herbert L. and William H. Taylor. *The America's Cup Races*. Princeton, New Jersey: D. Van Nostrand Company, Inc., 1958.

Swintal, Diane and R. Steven Tsuchya and Robert Kaimins. *Winging It, Oracle Team USA's Incredible Comeback To Defend the America's Cup*. Camden, Maine: International Marine/McGraw Hill Education, LLC. 2014

Waugh, Alec. *The Lipton Story. A Centennial Biography*. Garden City, New York: Doubleday & Company, Inc., 1950.

Whipple, A.B.C. *The Racing Yachts*. Alexandria, Virginia: Time-Life Books, 1980.

# INDEX